*Frontispiece: Smiling Balinese girls with flowers used for adornment and religious purposes in their daily life.*
*Pages 4-5: Sweeping rice terraces make a majestic icon of an agricultural nation.*
*Page 6: The kuda lumping or hobbyhorse trance dance of East Java is an astounding sight where entranced dancers paw the ground and behave like horses.*
*Pages 8-9: The grace of Bali's legong dancers belongs to the young. They retire by the time they reach puberty.*

## PHOTO CREDITS

All photographs in this book are from **Photobank** except for the following: pages 18, 20 (top), 22, 23 (centre and bottom), 30 (centre), 36 (top right), 37 (bottom), 43 (bottom right), 45 (top, bottom left and centre), 52 (bottom), 62 (top right), 63 (top left and bottom), 64 (top left and centre), 67, 68 (top centre, centre and centre right, bottom far left), 69 (bottom right), 72 (bottom left), 76 (top left), 77, 78 (top and centre), 79 (bottom left and right), 82 (bottom left), 83, 90, 91 (top left and right), 92 (top and centre left), 93 (top, centre and bottom right), 106 (bottom), 108 (centre right), 109, 110 (top left), 113 (bottom left and right), 118 (top left and centre), 121 (top right, centre left bottom), 125 (top and bottom), **Jill Gocher**; 10, 11, 12-13, 23 (top left), 24, 34 (bottom right), 35, 97, 108 (top), 127 (centre left, centre right bottom), **Focus Team–Italy**; 4-5, 15, 16 (top left), 17, 28, 84 (bottom right), 91 (bottom right), 95 (bottom), 113 (top and centre left), 124, 126, 127 (top and bottom), **Renata Holzbachová/Philippe Bénet**; 27 (bottom left), 29 (top and bottom right), 31 (top left and right), 57 (top row, centre), 94 (bottom left), 108 (centre left), 110 (bottom right), **Carl-Bernd Kaehlig**; 68 (bottom centre), 69 (left and centre right), 70 (centre right and bottom), 71, 72 (top left), **Robby Payne**; 38 (top left and right), 62 (bottom), 65 (centre left), 94 (top left), 110 (bottom left), 115 (top left), **Christine Osborne Pictures**; 74 (top right, bottom left and right), 118 (top left and bottom right), 127 (centre top right), **Hans Hayden**; 1, 79 (top left), 98 (centre) **Hutchison Library**; 94 (top and centre left), 95 (top right), **HBL Network**; 43 (bottom left), 79 (top right), **Richard l'Anson**; 2, 68 (far top right), **The Image Bank**; 37 (top centre and right), **John Maier Jr**; 69 (top right), **Bes Stock**.

INDONESIA: THE LAST PARADISE

© 1997 Times Editions Pte Ltd

Published by Times Editions
an imprint of Times Editions Pte Ltd
Times Centre, 1 New Industrial Road
Singapore 536196

Series Editor: K E Tan
Designer: Tuck Loong
Picture Researcher: Susan Jane A. Manuel
Production Manager: Anthoney Chua
Colour separation by Eray Scan Pte Ltd, Singapore
Printed in Singapore

ISBN: 981 204 037 4

*Sir,*
*Everytime u open this book, DO Remember us.. u are a good person to know, & surely to work with..*
*Bottom line is we'll miss you. "Take care.*
*-Dilah-*

*7. It's great great moment working with you and for a lot of reason.. I'm thank you...*
*-IWAN-*

*Pak Mark.*
*Success always yooo!*
*Faizn*

Mark
It has been a pleasure and privilege working with you this 3 years. I wish you success in the future [signature]

# INDONESIA
## THE LAST PARADISE

Hope that "Indonesia" will be in your memory forever.
— Melly —

MARK,
IT IS A PLEASURE TO SPEND A TIME WITH YOU. I THINK I STILL NEED YOUR ASSISTANCE IN THE NEXT FUTURE. HOPELY I CAN STILL CONTACT YOU.
WARM REGARDS,
— EMIL —

Mr. Mark.
Wish u all the best. Good luck. — Yosep —

Mark,
Many thanks for your assistance in the past to me best wishes for you in the future. Kind [signature]

Mark, Best of luck... MEGI

Mark
IT HAS BEEN A REAL PLEASURE WORKING AND PLAYING WITH YOU AND I HOPE WE CAN DO IT AGAIN SOMETIME SOON. BEST WISHES TO YOU AND JACOBI FOR THE FUTURE.
NCW 18-FEB-08

It was great working with you, hope you get all you are looking for in the future.
Dave Evans

I hope you have a good time in your new position. Thanks for all the help you gave me in the short time we have worked together
Chris Taylor.

Mark,
it's great to be part of your team. Thank you for all your knowledge sharing. Wish you all the best.
Agus Supjianto

It's been a great pleasure working with you. I've learnt a lot from you. I hope in the future I can learn a lot more.
Edi Putra.

Sir,
Best wishes for your future. It's been a pleasure knowing you and working with you. And definitely you're gonna be miss. Hope to see you again...
— Sifa —

Mark,
It was great and challenging working with you. The durable memories are the good ones.
Tony

Mr MARK,
GOOD LUCK AND GOD BLESS U
[signature]

Sir, Good luck...
— Plen —

MARK,
This is a proof that I CRIED when I heard you're leaving us (Hohoho) Good luck MR. Nice Guy!
[signature]

Don't forget us
GUDOMO

Mark,
It's been a pleasure to work together w/ you. I am sure that you will always remember how Siemens act.
DARMONO

Mr. Mark,
Good luck.
Adit

Mark, it was nice to be in your team. I hope you always be success in the future.
Kim H.

Mr. Brandbrook
I know you personally in the short time, however you give me many knowledge how handle important tasks for the project.
Thanks a lot.
See you next time : (Agung BW)

It's been great days worked with you. I hope to have rich chance in next future. Wish you & your great life & adventure! [signature]

Good luck to you, Hopely we can working together someday
NRG

Mark, Success for your future thank you for your kindness and share your experience to me
— HARSI —

Mark
We thank you for advise your experiences
[signature]

Mark,
semoga sukses selalu...
— nadia 18-2-2008

MARK,
WISH YOU ALL THE BEST. THANK YOU FOR PATIENT AND YOU ASSISTANCE. GOOD LUCK
— YAQUB —

Mark,
It was great and very nice working with the best partner like you. Hopely we can working together with you.
Zen.

Good luck Mr. Mark
[signature]

# INDONESIA
## THE LAST PARADISE

Text
JILL GOCHER

Photographs
PHOTOBANK
LUCA INVERNIZZI TETTONI
KAL MULLER

and others

TIMES EDITIONS

# CONTENTS

# INTRODUCTION

Look beyond the busy facades of Indonesia's modern cities with their towering office blocks, beyond the teeming streets choking with traffic and fumes, the air-conditioned cars replete with dark smoky-glass windows, their handphones and deal-making occupants. Look beyond these frenetic rhythms of an emerging technocratic nation, and listen carefully—beyond the cities there beat other, more ancient rhythms.

These spice-scented islands situated at Southeast Asia's southernmost extremes are an ethnic melting pot—the culmination of myriad migrations and invasions since the beginning of time. Over the ages, Indonesia became a treasure house of diverse cultures, of arts and people and of landscapes richer and more varied perhaps than any other country in the world.

Later arrivals brought cultures and skills complementing more ancient ones. The Hindus brought artistic styles and a sophisticated civilisation that suffused Java and beyond, bringing their religion to both the powerful Srivijaya and Majapahit empires. They created the mysterious temple complex of Dieng Plateau and the architectural masterpiece of Prambanan. The Buddhists brought the middle way and the great monument of Borobodur. Precious spices lured Arab traders who brought Islam to the islands along with their trade, while wandering Sufi mystics brought a gentler version of the religion, seducing rajahs and princes with their esoteric vision of the world.

From island to island the faces of the people change along with the landscape. The courtly dignity of the Javanese aristocrats gives way to the flamboyant pageantry of the Balinese. To the east, people show another heritage. The inhospitable, jungled mountains of Irian Jaya shelter communities of stone age tribesmen, while the Dayaks of Kalimantan have yet another face. The great diversity of people is united only by the thread of a national language and a strong national ideology expressed in the *Pancasila*.

The diversity is apparent too, in the ever changing landscape dominated by a string of over 500 volcanoes that sculpt the land, influencing profoundly the lives of the people that live beneath them. The volcanoes enrich the land, enough to keep it producing crop after crop of rice, up to three times a year, enough to feed the millions of lives that depend on this land for sustenance.

The rhythms of this great land are many. Outside the cities, time proceeds as it always did; unattached to the mechanics of industry, it is regulated by the rise and fall of the sun and the moon, the patterns of wind and rain. It is the rhythm of day and night, the rhythm of the seasons that have power. The benign climate and fertile lands of the main islands together with the almost clockwork regularity of the monsoon rains provide a living—for most, without great hardship.

Yet above all, it is the indomitable vitality of its people that provides the key to this nation's attraction. Described by Thomas Stamford Raffles, as "amiable and ingenious", the Indonesian people make any encounter in this magical country an indelible experience.

*In Bali, religion and life are inextricably entwined. Left: Costumed in traditional dress, these girls await the festivities of the Odalan ceremony. Above: Meru shrines of Bali's Pura Taman Ayun silhouetted against the setting sun. Following pages: Women laden with offerings at a village Odalan festival.*

# HISTORY AND THE INDONESIANS

Indonesia's rich and varied history dates back more than one and a half million years, to the time when prehistoric man walked the plains of Central Java at the beginning of the Pleistocene Age. These early men, known as *Homo erectus*, were a precursor to modern man, similar to a species who inhabited parts of China, Africa and Europe. They lived in caves hunting and gathering food where they found it and used primitive stone tools of choppers, axes and adze. Later in Java, near the royal town of Solo, a more advanced version of *Homo erectus*, dating from the late Pleistocene Age, was discovered in the 1930s. Solo Man as he was called, was hailed by scientists as the "missing link" between prehistoric and modern man.

Newcomers to the archipelago made their way through a series of migrations that occurred between 1500 and 2500 B.C. from the civilisations around the Indus and Mekong rivers, the Yangtze Kiang and the Irrawaddy, and remnants of neolithic cultures remain almost intact in various remote parts of Indonesia until today. Yet even while the neolithic and megalithic cultures creating magnificent stone monuments to their ancestral spirits were in existence, and the first agriculturalists were planting taro and other simple crops, the Bronze Age came to Indonesia in the form of finely wrought bronze Dong Son drums brought from North Vietnam, perhaps as early as 2,000 years B.C. These drums have lasted until today and are still used as ceremonial paraphernalia and as part of the bride price throughout the eastern islands of Indonesia.

Indonesia's unique geography too, plays an important part in its history—a history of great maritime empires whose fleets ruled the seas. By the seventh century, a Buddhist kingdom of no ordinary dimensions was established on the south Sumatran coast, somewhere near present-day Palembang. Srivijaya grew to such prominence that its rule lasted for six centuries, its influence stretching to Malaya and southern Thailand. All passing ships paid taxes and Srivijaya's ships, the biggest on the seas, sailed regularly to China and India, linking the countries to Sumatra with trade. Much of the trade was in precious commodities of gold, silk and porcelain in exchange for the equally precious commodities of cloves, pepper and mace from the eastern islands.

Java was the site of other inland empires, its fertile soils the spawning grounds for wet-rice agriculture and birthplace of a number of Hinduised kingdoms. One of the first known great temple-builders was the Hindu ruler Sanjaya, who was later replaced by the mysterious Sailendra kings, the builders of the great Buddhist monuments of Borobodur, Candi Mendut, Kalasan and Sewu. But the Sailendra's influence lasted less than one hundred years, to be replaced in A.D. 856 by Rakai Pikatan, a descendant of Sanjaya, who proceeded to erect the magnificent Loro Jonggrang temple at Prambanan.

*Massive poster artworks decorate Jakarta with one of the predominating images, that of the nation's President Suharto (left). The Proclamation of Independence Monument honouring Indonesia's first president, Soekarno, and his nationalist compatriot, Mohammad Hatta (above), is visited daily by groups of schoolchildren.*

Mysteriously, around A.D. 930, the centre of rule shifted to East Java. There under the rule of King Airlangga, who came to power in 1019, the flowering of Javanese culture took place. It was during the reign of this ascetic and patron of the arts that the famous *Arjuna Wiwaha* Sanskrit classics was translated into Javanese. After him a succession of capable rulers, helped in part by a strong economy based on agriculture, ensured the prosperity and stability that led to the formation of the new Majapahit Kingdom.

The Javanese too, became master mariners and by the middle of the 14th century, under the rule of King Hayam Wiruk and his chief minister Gajah Mada, the influence of Majapahit spread to the whole of Java and then the Indonesian archipelago. But following the death of Gajah Mada in 1364 and Hayam Wiruk in 1389, Majapahit's power started to wane considerably. Islam had entered the picture with a number of new states like Demak emerging along Java's northern coast. Political control of the coast was lost to the Muslims who later took over Java's central rice-producing areas, causing the entire aristocracy and court of the Majapahits to flee to Bali.

It was the wandering mystic Sufis who reinforced and amplified the words of Islam, brought first by Arab and Indian traders. Setting out to the world after Baghdad's fall, their mystic teachings, their poetry and dance and refined asceticism settled well with local aristocrats already attuned to ancient animistic beliefs, Brahmin Hindu advisors and tantric Buddhist dharma. For the local merchants, entering Islam was additionally attractive as it opened up a whole new brotherhood of international trade. Islam settled over Java not by war and fighting but as a gentle cloak of just one more layer of beliefs.

The 15th century witnessed the appearance of the colonising powers of Europe. All the explorer nations of renaissance Europe were to make their way to Indonesia, starting with the Portuguese, and later the Dutch and English, each bringing another set of Western values. It was Indonesia's fabulous spices and their promise of great fortunes that first attracted the Europeans. While the Arabs, Indians and Chinese had been trading there for centuries, it was not until Vasco da Gama rounded the Cape of Good Hope in 1497 that the first Europeans made their way to the East by sea.

While the Portuguese were the first European to set foot in Indonesia in 1509, they met with little success in entering the Islam-controlled spice trade. It was the Dutch however who were to establish a firm foothold on the archipelago. As their first ill-fated expedition to the Spice Islands limped back to Holland in 1597 to realise a small profit from the meagre cargo of spices they managed to bring home, it was to spark off the Spice Rush. In the following year, 22 ships were dispatched to the Indies.

*Indonesia's history is dotted with colonial figures, some of whom like Jan Pieterszoon Coen (top left) were noted more for their ruthlessness than humanitarianism. Top right, below: Batavia during Coen's time. Top right, above: The island of Banda Neira was once the hub of the spice trade, considered so valuable by the Dutch that they exchanged Manhattan Island with the British for it.*

A consortium of merchants known as the United East India Company or VOC was established, under the aegis of the Dutch government, to manage this lucrative trade and the riches that go with it. The VOC had a singular business philosophy—monopoly. They wanted it all and they wanted control.

In 1614, a Dutchman named Jan Pieterszoon Coen decided that a more forceful policy would make trade more profitable for the Dutch. After taking command of the VOC, he set out to establish a permanent base in Jayakarta (modern Jakarta) close to Banten and the Sunda Straits. From there he started a campaign of conquest of the spice islands of the Banda Group, transforming the islands into a slave colony.

The Dutch didn't stop there. The clove islands of Ternate and Tidore were next to receive their attention and in 1649 a series of sweeps of the area was made to stop any unauthorised clove traders. The sweeps were so successful that half the islanders starved while the rest were reduced to abject poverty.

All the bitter fighting and bloodshed led to the eventual control of the Indies for the VOC, but due to the great greed and corruption in Java, it all ended in ignominy when in 1799 the VOC was announced to be bankrupt and quietly disbanded. In 1800, the Netherlands government took over all the former possessions of the ill-fated VOC putting H.W. Daendels in command. Daendel's rule was soon interrupted by the aftermath of the Napoleonic Wars and the British put T.S. Raffles in charge in 1811. During his five years of rule, Raffles tried to put the country to rights with the introduction of enlightened new policies, taxes and a free trade system. But even before it was properly in place, the Dutch returned in 1816.

Raffles' bright new laws were reinterpreted, to the advantage of the Dutch, leading to even worse times for the people. For the next hundred years or so, much of the Indonesian population were working for next to nothing and suffering great hardship. These bitterly hard times spawned heroes like Javanese Prince Diponegoro (1785-1855) who led a series of revolts against the Dutch, which ended in his capture and incarceration beneath the strong stone walls of the fort in Makassar.

Part of this history is written in the spilled blood of the national heroes who gave their lives for a greater vision. While nationalism got off to a slow start, change was on the way. By the early 20th century, Indonesians were beginning to receive a Dutch education, providing a basis for nationalism. Regional study organisations were set up spawning a group of new Indonesian leaders, which led to the famous Youth Pledge of 1928, proclaiming the concept of "One people, One language, One nation".

An Islamic movement began to grow and rallies attracted over 50,000 people. A communist party too was formed and from 1910 to 1930 a growing number of strikes pointed to workers' unrest. In 1927, a young student named Soekarno in conjunction with his Bandung Study Club formed the first political party—its goal? Independence for Indonesia. A series of misadventures followed, and Soekarno after being arrested several times was exiled to eastern Indonesia. But it didn't stop there.

It was the Japanese who inadvertently helped the cause of nationalism. During the years of World War Two they found it necessary to rely on Indonesian assistance, placing them in key positions previously held by the Dutch. Nationalists were freed. As the war drew to a close, and it became ap-

parent that the Japanese were losing, they encouraged nationalism leading to greater strengthening of an Indonesian consciousness.

Just days after the second atomic bomb dropped on Hiroshima on 17th August 1945, Soekarno and his nationalist compatriot Mohammad Hatta, proclaimed *Merdeka*—independence for the nation and an end to tyranny. As the news spread, cries of *"Merdeka!"* could be heard echoing through the streets, and the beginnings of a new nation was born.

On the fifth anniversary of the proclamation, after five more years of bitter struggle and heroic sacrifices of the people, Indonesia was declared a Republic.

*Indonesia has given birth to numerous heroes like Prince Diponegoro (top), who defied family and friends to fight for his country's freedom. Bottom: Mohammad Hatta (sitting at right) who fought long and hard for Indonesia's independence became the country's first Vice President.*

# PART ONE
# THE LAND

**B**orn of the fire of countless volcanoes, refreshed with the deluging waters of tropical storms and nourished by the strong sun, the Indonesian archipelago forms an extravagant mosaic of tropical colours, gleaming in a palette of every imaginable hue.

From the deep emerald greens of the jungle to the iridescent greens of growing padi, the colours shift to the cerulean and aquamarine of waters surrounding coral islands, to dazzling azure skies and the deep obsidian of night. The brilliant gold of a tropical sunrise gives way to the misty purples of distant mountains, to the electric reds, pinks and oranges of myriad tropical blooms and technicolour sunsets so spectacular that the sky is left glowing in astonishment.

The mosaic embodies some of the most diverse landscapes of our planet—a full spectrum of tropical habitats. The equatorial rain forests that cover parts of Sumatra and Borneo form a vivid contrast to Java and Bali's spectacularly fertile rice lands with their majestic outlines of smoking volcanic cones. The open grass savannah plains of Nusa Tenggara changes to the permanent snowcaps of Irian Jaya's mountains—the highest peaks between the Andes and the Himalayas. Between are Maluku's (the Moluccas) coral encircled islands of white sand and coconut trees and the turquoise fantasies of unexplored coral reefs beyond, denoting paradise in any language.

Much of the landscape is shaped by nature, the sum total of eons of shifting surfaces, of three tectonic plates colliding, reforming and reshaping the land. These violent times result in earthquakes and tidal waves as the land reestablishes its equilibrium. Vast coral ridges pressed up from the seabed to become mountains while deep troughs were formed. Living volcanoes exert the twin threats of powerful destruction even while creating new life and abundant fertility in this geologically young land.

Yet too, the landscape is shaped by man in his eternal struggle for survival. Outside the sprawling cities, in the *desa* or villages, attachment to the land is paramount, a harmony of man and his environment at ease with natural forces. Like the taming of the wild buffalo, man has learned to live with the land, gently shaping it to his will.

In traditional eyes, nature is a powerful force that must be respected. Villages and settlements are constructed with great heed to the surroundings and to ignore them would invite disaster. In Sulawesi's remote Torajaland, village houses are oriented to the north, while in Yogyakarta, the *kraton* (palace) faces towards ferocious Mt. Merapi, the giver and taker of life and source of great energy.

Over the millennia in Bali and Java, man has learned how to harness nature's abundance with sophisticated irrigation systems that ensure each farmer's enjoyment of the precious water supply. The spectacular mountain terraces of Bali, Sulawesi and Java belie the infinite care and patience which man employs to make the landscape work for him, digging and building and shaping the land to incredible proportions, while respecting and retaining the natural order.

*I*ndonesia's natural beauty overwhelms the senses. Left: Bali's verdant rice fields can leave you breathless.
Above: Ulu Watu's steep cliffs attract surfers to some of the best waves on Bali.

# A PATTERN OF ISLANDS

From the air, Indonesia's 13,667 islands sprawl below like a string of precious jewels, stretching over 5,120 kilometres of tropical sea from east to west, nearly one eighth of the earth's circumference. While the number of islands is immense, they are not all small tropical paradise style islands at all. Indeed Indonesia is also the proud possessor of some of the world's largest islands, which include Sumatra, Borneo (Kalimantan on the Indonesian side), Irian Jaya and Sulawesi.

The islands of this new land are still forming. In remote atolls off the coasts of Sumatra and deep in the heart of the Maluku seas, dim outlines of new islands can be seen emerging from the sea.

*Indonesia's islands come in all shapes and forms. Centre: Bali's holy Pura Tanah Lot is an island off the island, a mecca both for devout Balinese and hordes of tourist who flock there each evening. Left: The fishing boats of Bali come highly decorated*

*T*he Outer Islands are less inhabited than Bali and Java, with a charm all their own.
Top left: A long deserted beach on Sulawesi's west coast is enjoyed by local fishermen.
Top right: Komodo Island is surrounded by sweeping seas where treacherous currents
have long kept unwanted predators at bay, preserving the habitat of the prehistoric
Komodo dragons.

# Life on the Outer Islands

While life in the major cities of Bali, Java and parts of Sumatra is fast-paced, with a strong Western flavour, tempered by centuries of outside influences and foreign visitors, it is still uniquely Indonesian. But on the more remote islands, far from the tourist trail, or world television, where outside influence has barely penetrated, life takes on different textures as traditional ways hold communities together.

The daily life of the people follows patterns that have evolved over the centuries and in some parts it is difficult to believe it is still the twentieth century. Age-old formulas for building unique houses, rearing cattle, weaving cloth, producing pottery, conducting a wedding ceremony are adhered to, preserving the *adat* (code of conduct and traditional practices) for future generations. Every passage of life from birth to puberty and death are marked by ceremonies and rituals.

*In the arid Lesser Sunda Islands, the* lontar *palm provides most neccessities of life (top right). Collected daily, the sap from the leaves feeds babies and when fermented, makes an alcoholic brew enjoyed by young and old.*

*The distinctive roofs of a traditional Sumba village emerge through the trees (top left). Facing page: In Sumba, home-grown cotton is spun by hand before dyeing and weaving into ikat blankets. Centre left: No electric machines means that all things are produced using age-old methods like this man making flour. Left: A sudden downpour brings a burst of activity on Pulau Tanimbar Kei. When there is no umbrella, a banana leaf suits the purpose perfectly well (above). Centre right: A fisherman and his son return home, paddling across the vast seas of Maluku.*

*F*ishing styles vary across the archipelago. Right: These fishermen cast a net from their dugout perahu in the shallow waters off the islands.

*D*ays in Flores villages are filled with traditional activities. Top left: Games of combat form important rites of passage and trials of manhood in village life. Top right: Terraced padi fields are worked in the traditional way maximising use of available land. Above: Ceremonial dance varies even from village to village. Right: The art of ikat weaving in Flores is highly developed. Far right: Basketry is another of Flores' specialty.

In spite of encroaching "civilisation" from other islands, life in Irian Jaya's Baliem Valley follows age-old ways with customs and traditions barely changed for centuries. Left: When American adventurer Richard Archibold discovered the Baliem Valley in the 1930s, he was amazed to find rows of gardens laid out as neatly as "any market gardens in Europe". Far left: Hunting parties take little but the bare necessities of life and a bundle of spears on their trips. Below: Dani tribesmen with their prize catch.

The people of Irian Jaya are very keen on body adornment and men will spend hours preening themselves before any special occasion. Left: A fine specimen of a Dani warrior in Irian Jaya's Baliem Valley. Far right: An elegant blend of the traditional and modern. Right: The womenfolk wear a variety of simple clothing forms.

# Indonesia's Teeming Seas

Few parts of Indonesia are far from the sea which comprises more than two thirds of this scattered nation. Indonesia's 3.1 million square kilometres of water mass provides a livelihood for millions across the archipelago.

The lateen-rigged sails of countless fishing boats take to the seas each morning, to return with hauls of gleaming silver fish and other stranger marine creatures. Parts of the archipelago lie in the migratory paths of the big fish such as the marlin, mackeral, sailfish and tuna, fish worth almost a king's ransom in rich developed nations like Japan, Taiwan or Hong Kong. The outlying islands to the east with their surrounding reefs are home to exotic fish and marine life which also find their way to the tables of the rich.

The sea has also been the conduit for many factors that have shaped the life of the islanders. Newer migratory groups came to Indonesia via the sea, adding their cultures and skills to an ever growing diversity. The spice trade too was facilitated first by inter-island trade and then later by foreign traders and explorers who brought the new religions of first Buddhism and Hindu, and later Islam and to a lesser extent, Christianity, to the islands.

*The* Mona Lisa *is readied for sail (above). All work on Indonesia's traditional Buginese schooner is manual.*

*In myriad ways, the sea provides a livelihood for many of Indonesia's people. Left: Basket of fish fresh from the fishing boats on the way to market. Centre: Whaling by harpoon is still practised on the small island of Lembata in East Nusa Tenggara. Above: Buginese schooners, part of one of the very few remaining sailing fleets in the world line up along Jakarta's Sunda Kelapa Harbour. Right: The sea relinquishes all kinds of marine life.*

# RING OF FIRE

Indonesia is right in the midst of the "Ring of Fire", a live volcanic region that arcs down from Sumatra to Java, Lombok, Sumbawa and Flores and northwards to Sulawesi, Maluku, and beyond to the Philippines and Japan, bending eastwards as far as Alaska and southwards down the coasts of the USA and South America.

With over 500 volcanoes scattered across the islands, about 38% of which are active, most Indonesians live within sight of a fiery mountain. Krakatau and Tambora were two of the world's most cataclysmic eruptions and the rollcall of melodious names, Merapi, Bromo, Rinjani, Papandayan, Agung and Sibayak seems to evoke their might. Perhaps the biggest and most destructive eruption of all happened at what is now Sumatra's Lake Toba. This prehistoric eruption, which happened some 75,000 years ago, created the largest lake in Southeast Asia and certainly, with a depth of around 450 metres, the deepest in the world.

Volcanic action is a two-edged sword—even as mountains spewed up hundreds of tonnes of ash and rock into the stratosphere destroying everything in their wake, they nuture the very place they destroy by renewing the land with new layers of nutrient-rich lava and ash, making parts of Indonesia one of the most fertile lands of the planet.

Living on such intimate terms with the fiery mountains, man has endowed the mountains with myths and legends and mystical powers that play a part in the daily lives of the people. Mountains are sources of power and homes to all kinds of living deities, especially in Java, Lombok and Bali.

*Volcanoes sculpt Indonesia's landscapes creating islands of fire, such as the Ile Api of Lembata (above). Violent eruptions create vast lakes of which Lake Toba (below) is the largest in Asia, or others, like the Keli Mutu lakes of Flores (bottom left) which change colours from the palest aquamarine to deep turquoise.*

*The people of Indonesia live under the shadow of erupting volcanoes their whole lives. Taking advantage of the fertile soil which produces several crops a year, villages are built high on the mountain slopes as in the Dieng Plateau (far right) and Wonosobo in Central Java (overleaf).*

# The Explosion Heard Around the World

In August 1883, the little volcanic island of Krakatau erupted with a bang that was heard around the world from Rangoon to Perth. After the first cataclysmic explosion caused the core to be ejected, the mountain collapsed upon itself, causing the sea water to rush in contacting with the molten lava and causing an even bigger explosion of truly memorable proportions. Over 21 cubic kilometres of rock and volcanic debris shot 26 kilometres into the air turning day into night for 160 kilometres in every direction. The resulting waves rose up to 40 metres, wiping out the whole coastline of West Java and the Sunda Straits, and stranding boats kilometres inland.

Tidal waves, triggered by the volcano's collapse, were recorded as far away as South America and Hawaii while the Indian Ocean was littered with tonnes of floating pumice. The ash and smoke that melted into the atmosphere changed the world's weather patterns and caused brilliant red sunsets for three years afterwards.

Forty-four years later, Anak Krakatau or "child of Krakatau" rose from the sea bed, first appearing as a small rocky cone. She stands quietly now with no more than an occasional rumble, puffs of white smoke issuing serenely from a growing peak that has already reached more than 150 metres.

# Mystical Home of the Gods

Dominating the whole eastern side of Bali is the cloud-swathed 3,142-metre peak of Gunung Agung, the holy mountain that is home to Bali's many deities who look down over their perfect island. High on the mountain slope is Pura Besakih, Bali's mother-temple complex that draws a constant procession of people throughout the year. During important festivals the Balinese come to pay tribute to the gods to make offerings and appease them with gifts of song and dance, for if the gods become angry, all hell breaks loose as they vent their displeasure with a volcanic eruption.

Every 100 years, the most special, most sacred ceremony is held within the temple's many compounds. The Eka Dasa Rudra festival is a ritualised purification of the universe given to drive off the evil spirits into the eleven sacred directions of the world. The festival's very name comes from the Sanskrit word, *eka desa*, meaning "eleven".

*Pura Besakih, Bali's mother-temple is located on the slopes of mystical Gunung Agung (top left), the island's holiest mountain. Celebrations and festivals are held all year (above) while the elaborate Eka Dasa Rudra (above right) is held once every hundred years, to restore harmony between man and nature. Intricate flower offerings (left and far left) are a vital part of every temple festival with prayers made to the gods (right).*

# Dante's Inferno

The desolate and otherworldly moonscape of Mt. Bromo lies in the heart of a vast caldera more than 10 kilometres in diameter. From the caldera rise the tips of four mountain peaks, while to the south is the smoking outline of Java's highest mountain, the 3,678-metre Mt. Semeru.

One of Indonesia's most popular tourist volcanic attraction, Mt. Bromo is part of the Tengger Mountains in East Java, a region inhabited by Hindus left over from the Majapahit Empire. Many beliefs and legends surround Mt. Bromo. Each year during the last month of the Tenggerese calendar, Tenggerese pilgrims reenact the story of Joko Seger who gave his life to save his descendants. By midnight thousands of believers have assembled in the Sea of Sand below the volcano, bearing offerings of money, vegetables, flowers, chickens and even goats. Amidst clouds of burning incense, 28 priests intone incantations, invoking the spirits of Siva and other guardian deities, who descend to the lower earthly realms to give blessings to the assembled throng. After completion of the rites, the growing crowd makes its way up the steep sides of the caldera to throw their offerings to the smoking crater below, assuring another year of peace and prosperity for all.

*The otherworldly atmosphere of Mt. Bromo (right) attracts visitors from around the world who rise long before dawn to cross the Sea of Sand on horseback (top right) in time to reach the caldera for a spectacular sunrise view (above). The caldera measures almost 10 kilometres in diameter. site of the most ancient eruption. Within the caldera, four small peaks rise from the central floor. While three are lush and overgrown. Mt. Bromo is dry and eerie—another world in the midst of Java's lush beauty.*

*T*he Tengger Highlands around Mt. Bromo support one of the few remaining Hindu communities and extant temples in Java (left). Each year on the 14th day of the month of Kesodo, the faithful make a pilgrimage to the mountain to bring offerings of live goats and chickens, fruit and flowers (above and right) to the god of the mountain.

# AGRICULTURE —THE HEART OF A NATION

*Agricultural wealth ranges from the millions of tonnes of rice to exotic cloves (right and below) to the beloved* salak *or snake fruit (above). While home-grown tobacco (bottom) comes from many islands including Java, Sumatra and Lombok and the arid islands to the east, it is the magnificent terraces of* padi *(facing page and overleaf) that form the most spectacular landscapes.*

In spite of burgeoning industrialisation, a massive oil industry and large-scale mineral productions, Indonesia is very much an agricultural nation. Four out of five people still work the soil, contributing over 20% of the gross domestic product.

While rice is the main crop and the mainstay of the nation, it is by no means the only important crop grown. Besides the other staples of sago, corn and the tuberous cassava, cash crops such as rubber, pepper, oil palm, coconut, clove, teak, sugar cane and cacao are grown in large quantities.

In the cool highland areas of Java, Bali and Sumatra vast areas of land are given over to the cultivation of fresh garden vegetables to feed the ever growing urban markets of the lowlands and to export to the nearby markets of Singapore and Malaysia.

## Java—The Rice Bowl of Indonesia

The main crop of the nation is rice, a crop that occupies a large part of the lives of many Indonesians. More than 50% of Javanese are rice farmers, following a tradition that has lasted for over 2,000 years.

Rice in Indonesia is so important that it enjoys an almost mystical quality. No meal is complete without rice and no honoured guest could ever be entertained without copious amounts of the fluffy white grain at hand. During the growth cycle, each stage is carefully monitored, likened to a pregnant woman. Celebrations, ritual feasts and festivities are held to commemorate the growing, harvesting, threshing and eating of this small white grain. Dewi Sri, the rice goddess, is paid great respect with effigies made in her honour.

Most productive of all Indonesia's rice-growing areas is Java—the nation's rice bowl where over 20% of all land is irrigated rice fields or *sawah*. Indonesian rice production has increased dramatically in recent years. From 1980, when the country was the world's biggest rice importer, new scientifically created high yield strains have seen production increase so dramatically that by 1991 rice production totalled over 44 million tonnes.

# Bali's Sophisticated Subak System

It is no miracle that all of Bali's incredible rice terraces receive sufficient irrigation water to nuture the young plants; it is the result of a system evolved over 1,000 years. Waters from the the island's more than 150 rivers and streams are directed by a series of weirs and subterranean tunnels, some over a kilometre long, that are cut into the soft volcanic rock. Then through pipelines and conduits they are directed to the rice fields.

It is then the job of water distribution that takes precedence. Intricate timing is required by each village whose *subak* organisation controls the flow. Every water-using farmer is a member of the community *subak* that regulates his fields. Each area has use of the water on a specified day that concurs with the *subak* member's calculations of the best planting times.

*Community self-help or* gotong-royong *keeps the agricultural system of Bali operating not only for water distribution, but also for harvesting padi (left). Farmers such as this (above) work in groups to shape the spectacular rice terraces and fields (centre and top) while ploughing is done with the aid of cows or buffaloes. Right: Javanese tea pickers work to fill large cane baskets, plucking only the tenderest of young leaves. When it rains, they return home.*

# Java's Tea Gardens

The cool highlands of Java and the rich volcanic soil provide the perfect climate for tea production. In 1994, around 170,000 tonnes were produced with 90,000 tonnes exported. The crop was first introduced from China by Dutchman J. Jacobson but was unsuccessful in Java's hot climate. Later, plants brought from Darjeeling in India by John Peet in 1878 proved successful, and the first commercial plantations were established near Bandung.

Many of the tea estates are scenic, their well-trimmed bushes issuing a bright green over the verdant hills. The gardens are beautifully maintained while the plantation colonial buildings are kept in perfect condition. Tea estates can be found spread across Java from Bogor and Puncak close to Jakarta to the highland areas around Bandung, Ciater and the Mt. Papandayan area.

# MAJESTIC RIVERS

For an island nation, a surprising number of rivers traverse the country and some are quite substantial. The rivers of Sumatra and Kalimantan alone total almost 16,500 kilometres, 10,437 kilometres being navigable with a depth of at least one metre during the dry season.

Rivers have long been important trade and communication routes. In most parts of the country, it was the coastal areas and along the river banks that were first settled. Many Indonesian ports are still located upriver—for example Samarinda and Banjarmasin in Kalimantan and in Sumatra, Jambi is 120 kilometres upstream while Palembang is 80 kilometres. Coastal areas were often unsuitable because of dense mangroves and swampy terrain, while upstream also afforded protection from the monsoons and shelter from maurauding traders.

In the interior regions of Indonesian Borneo, known as Kalimantan, rivers were once the only means of access to the interior. Directions were relegated by the terms, *hulu* and *hilir* or upriver and downriver, which are still in use today to describe remote places. Today while these riverine highways are being usurped by newly made roads cutting through what was once dense jungle, many still choose to use the waterways as a cheap and convenient means of transport.

*The interior of Indonesia's larger islands are dissected by intricate river systems which as they reach the flat lowlands, wind their way through the nipa jungle to the sea (above). Travel within the interior often relies on watery mode of transport such as this simple perahu (right).*

*Rivers act as highways to the interior and on smaller tributaries Dayak villages in Kalimantan straddle the rivers banks (right) to take advantage of this. Waterside stores, such as this (far right), supply goods to boat-borne customers while folks wash and bathe along the steep banks (above).*

# The Mahakam

One of Kalimantan's greatest rivers, the Mahakam winds its way from the swampy lowlands, up to the very depths of Borneo. The broad lower reaches which can measure up to five kilometres across are a major waterway. Navigable all year round, the river accommodates ocean-going ships to venture up as far as the historic trading town of Samarinda. Wildlife too is diverse in the lower reaches which are home to freshwater dolphins and man-eating crocodiles that hide in the river's many tributaries.

As the river gains elevation and rapids appear, transportation becomes more difficult. The river boats and motorised craft give way to smaller sampans and speedboats until as the river narrows and rapids increase in size, it is only the purpose-built indigenous longboats that can forge their way upstream.

As the river narrows, the isolated towns and communities too, become smaller until it is a series of timber longhouses, homes to many Dayak tribes who have lived there for centuries. A strong downriver migration has been occurring over the last few years as the river people come in search of education, jobs and modern amenities, yet in many of the smaller tributaries, tribal life continues much as it ever did.

*Bamboo provides easy transportation when tied together and rafted downstream (above) from the longhouses of the interior (top) to the coastal markets. It is also a popular form of transportation in rural Sulawesi (above centre). The river makes a rent-free venue for the floating markets found in Banjarmasin (right) and other centres in South Kalimantan.*

# PART TWO

# FLORA AND FAUNA

Tigers, elephants, orangutans and rhinoceros, birds of paradise, cockatoos, coloured parrots and rhinoceros hornbills, orchids, rafflesia and butterflies—Indonesia is a cornucopia of exotic animals and plants. There is almost no limit to Indonesia's incredibly rich wildlife where open plains and lush equatorial jungles are inhabited by 500 species of mammals and 1,600 species of birds. Plant species are almost uncountable.

In the nineteenth century, when Victorian naturalist and evolutionist Alfred Russel Wallace was wandering the Malay Archipelago collecting data for his book, *The Malay Archipelago*, he described Java as "the very Garden of the East and perhaps, upon the whole, the richest...tropical island in the whole world."

The archipelago is a collecting point, a transition zone where the species of both Asiana in the west and Australasia to the east inhabit the scattered islands. As the world evolved, and icecaps covered the northern and southern latitudes, water levels plummeted causing shallow seas to recede, joining islands and allowing easy animal migrations between the Asian landmasses.

As he explored eastwards, Wallace noted the distinct differences in the flora and fauna between the eastern and western islands remarking in his book, "If we look at a map of the Archipelago nothing seems more unlikely than that the closely related chain of islands from Java to Timor should differ materially in their natural productions."

Yet during his travels, he discovered there was a difference and the differences between Bali and Lombok, separated by a narrow strait of just a few kilometres, were especially noticeable. Where Bali was populated by Asian animals, Lombok was inclined towards Austronesian. Wallace marked a line between the islands declaring Bali and Borneo to be the eastern limit of Asiana. It became known as the Wallace Line and the country to the east became known as Wallacia.

Left out of the past few ice ages for over a million years, the flora and fauna of the Indonesian archipelago have evolved undisturbed and over 800 species are endemic, found nowhere else in the world. Of all the islands, Sulawesi is the most diverse, a "Noah's Ark" of endemic plant and animal species.

An astonishing array of wildlife runs from the tiniest insects to the game animals that inhabit the equatorial rain forests of the archipelago—the leopards, elephants, tigers and rhinoceros, found deep within the shaded confines. Almost human orangutans live high in the forest canopy, rarely ever descending to the lower levels and the ground, each occupying its own little piece of territory.

Ubiquitous leaf monkeys which are found all over Western Indonesia share the jungle with wild black Celebes monkeys and the red-haired, pot-bellied Proboscis monkeys with its human-like nose, nick-named "Belanda" (or Hollander) by a whimisical population. The exotic bird life once attracted traders from China and Europe who came to buy the birds of paradise as decorations for the clothes of the rich.

*While industrialisation encroaches on the natural habitat of Indonesia's flora and fauna, the endangered orangutan (left) continues to beguile all who come into contact with it. The pig-tail macaque (above), which can still be found in many parts of the Sumtaran jungle, is often domesticated and trained to pluck coconuts for humans.*

# FACE OF THE EQUATORIAL RAIN FOREST

Much of Indonesia is still covered with tropical rain forest containing numerous tree species, flowering fruit trees, ferns, orchids and abundant animal life. The rain forest encompasses its own eco-system, a heavily interdependent chain of actions that cause each component to contribute to the survival of the next. While the actual soil is nutrient-poor, leached by heavy rainfalls of the equatorial belt, the hot tropical climate causes plant matter to decay quickly, adding nutrients back to the soil. The trees and their roots together with the land covering of mushy decomposing leaves acts as a natural sponge holding and retaining the abundant moisture from the heavy rainfall. Water runoff from virgin forest is generally clear rather than the muddy flow from sadly deforested land.

But as the demands of development are increasingly destroying natural habitats in parts of the country, huge tracts of virgin land have been put aside as national parks and nature reserves. Even in Java, one of the world's most crowded islands, there is space for several areas of complete wilderness.

Twenty-four national parks had been gazetted by 1991, encompassing an area of 6.9 million hectares, many in areas of complete wilderness and three have been adopted by the IUCN as World Heritage Sites. That is the Komodo National Park in Nusa Tenggara, Java's Ujung Kulon, the last refuge of the Javan rhinoceros and the Lore Lindu National Park in Sulawesi.

## Bogor's Botanical Riches

Spreading out along the lower reaches of Mt. Salak is Bogor's world famous Kebun Raya or Botanic Gardens, once the finest in Asia. Established by the Dutch in 1817, under the directorship of Professor C.G.C. Reinwardt, and his assistants, James Hooper and William Rent, all from Britain's Kew Gardens, the 87-hectare gardens contain over 15,000 species of tropical plants from around the world, including 400 palm species and 3,000 varieties of orchid. The Kebun Raya is also used for research purposes and it is here that much of the early work was done on cash crops of rubber, tea, cassava, tobacco and coffee, and on the medicinal properties of cinchona (quinine). It is also the site of one of Asia's first oil palms brought from Africa in 1848.

*In many parts of Indonesia, the tropical rain forest remains in near pristine condition (facing page). Above and left: The Cibodas and Bogor botanical gardens were once the best in Asia, the research grounds for new species being introduced for commercial plantations.*

# INDONESIA'S UNIQUE SPECIES

I ndonesia is probably the most diverse nation in our world and a haven for lovers of statistics. While occupying only 1.3% of the world's land surface, the country occupies a far higher percentage in the world's annals of flora and fauna. Ten per cent or 25,000 of the world's flowering plants can be found here, as can 17% or 1,600 of bird species, 12% or 500 of mammals and an astonishing 25% or 8,500 of the world's marine life.

Even more compelling is the knowledge that 816 endemic species are found between its shores including 310 mammals, 356 birds and 150 reptiles. Some of the more interesting of the endemic species include Sulawesi's unique Maleo bird, a hen-sized megapod that lays an egg the size of an ostrich. Not only is the egg enormous, but after hatching and struggling from its warm pit the baby bird is able to fly immediately. The primitive Komodo Dragon with its poisonous breath inhabits the far reaches of Nusa Tenggara while the superbly feathered Bird of Paradise lives in the deep jungles of New Guinea.

*Some Indonesian species have unexpected attributes like the noses of Sulawesi's endemic tube-nosed bat (right) and Kalimantan's quirky Proboscis monkey (above) whose protruding nose and bulging stomach earned it the moniker of "Belander" or "Hollander".*

*Prowling deep within the jungle, the steadily decreasing numbers of Sumatran tiger (above) continue to instil terror into the hearts of any man or beast who comes across them, including this rare Sumatran mountain goat (left) who is however nimble enough to skip out of harm's way.*

## The World's Largest Bloom

The Stinking Corpse Lily, Devil's Betel Box and Sun Toadstool are just some of the rather unattractive names the Indonesians give to the world's largest bloom that lives within the deep jungles of Sumatra and Borneo.

The Rafflesia is named after Thomas Stamford Raffles, who discovered it with botanist Dr Joseph Arnold during Raffles' sojourn as governor of Bengkulu. The bloom of this inimitable plant can measure up to almost one metre across for the *Rafflesia arnoldii*, the largest variety.

The red flower blossoms only for a few short days, attracting flies and other insects with its lively aroma of rotting carrion to assist with pollination. This parasitic plant comes with no stem, no leaves or roots of any kind, merely a few fungal strands that exist within the host plant, a vine-like creeper known as *Tetrastigma*. The flower can take up to two years to blossom, and after a bud appears, will take another two to three months to flower.

*Many islands support endemic species. The distinctive black and white colouring of this Sumatran tapir (top left) is an effective form of camouflage while the Sulawesi crested black macaque (top right) is so fiercesome, he needs no camouflage at all. Left: The glowing red of a Rafflesia flower in full bloom lasts no more than a few days before it dissolves back into the jungle floor that spawned it.*

# Face to Face with a Komodo Dragon

When old-time mariners returned from voyages to the Spice Islands they came back with tales of fearsome fire-breathing dragons; yet for years afterwards the dragons could not be found. Deadly, turbulent currents encircled the islands of Komodo and Rinca keeping all but the most hardy fishermen away and inadvertently preserving the prehistoric dragons, which otherwise would surely have been lost to the world.

Fired by fear, the imagination of these ancient mariners transformed the reptiles' flickering tongues to fire, but in reality, the tongues are the Komodos' key sensor. With poor eyesight and hearing, the dragons rely on their forked tongue to test the air for strange odours and the scent of their favourite meal—the wild deer and goats that live on their islands.

These Komodo Dragons (*Varanus komodoensis*) that live in the Komodo National Park can grow up to three metres in length and weigh up to 80 kilograms.

Now preservation is assured. The islands form part of a national park and the animals are heavily protected. Tourism has also helped to preserve the creatures by giving them a monetary value. Previously, feedings were conducted for groups of tourists with freshly killed goats being brought to the site, but free food caused them to lose their natural hunting instincts. The males being stronger would take the lion's share of the food while the females became thinner, weaker and unable to breed. Now it's hunting season all year for the Komodos with severe penalties for anyone who tries to give them food.

*The Komodo dragons (right) live on only the three islands, Komodo, Rinca and Pada, which form the perimeters of the Komodo National Park. The dragons were once given a weekly feeding (above) for the edification of tourists but the practice has since been stopped. When feeding, the creatures' sharp teeth and claws (left) can tear up a live goat or deer in seconds.*

## The Increasingly Rare Javan Rhinoceros

Lurking in the deep forest of Java's most surprising wildlife refuge of Ujung Kulon are the last remaining specimens of the Javanese rhinoceros.

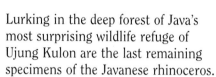

This elusive one-horned beast has been almost decimated in recent years, not least by the poachers hunting their extremely valuable horn. The Chinese believe it possesses aphrodisiacal properties and there is a big demand in the lucrative markets of Singapore, Hong Kong and Taiwan.

It is estimated that only 50 to 60 specimens of the once abundant creatures remain in the wilderness of this remote 510 square kilometres reserve in southern West Java and even many of the working rangers have spotted one only once or twice in their careers.

*Only 50 to 60 specimens of Java's unique rhinos remain in the wild, spurring increasing efforts by wildlife organisations to preserve the species habitat and introduce breeding programmes in an effort to increase their numbers. Top: A Javan rhino in the Ujung Kulon National Park. Above and centre: A photograph and drawing of a Sumatran rhino.*

# Rehabilitating the Orangutan

The friendly and lovable orangutan or "man of the jungle" who shares 96% of DNA make-up with human beings is our nearest relative. Once they roamed the jungles of Kalimatan Borneo and northern Sumatra but recently has run into difficult times. As logging increases, its habitat has become seriously denuded and many babies are orphaned as their mothers are killed in logging accidents.

Then there are the poachers who knowing just how good a price these creatures can fetch in the market will kill the mothers to take the infant. Owning an orangutan can be quite fashionable in certain circles too.

Young orangutans in lumber camps are taught to smoke cigarettes and drink beer, while others are kept chained in poor conditions with no food. Worst are those that are brought to the bars and discos of Bangkok and Taiwan where they are kept as party entertainment for the patrons.

The species is now on the endangered list with an estimated 5,000 remaining in the wild. Rehabilitation Centres have been set up in Tanjung Puting National Park in South Kalimantan and in Sumatra at Bukit Lawang in the Gunung Leuser National Park. The aim is to bring the animals back to the jungle and to teach them the jungle skills they lack.

# Lampung's Wild Elephants

Living in Sumatra, a still sizeable elephant population is at once a protected species and a nuisance. Arriving from the north, they are of a similar species to their cousins in Malaysia and northern Thailand.

Unfortunately, in the Lampung province men have come to live in their traditional lands, turning their jungles into agricultural plots, fencing them and blocking traditional migratory paths. The elephants are naturally upset at this disturbance to their routine and retaliate by tearing down the fences, destroying the houses and eating the crops.

The men get disturbed and retaliate by capturing the elephants and sending them to the reserve in Way Kambas where they are taught to play soccer and balance on tiny stools.

*With a DNA pattern more than 95% that of humans, orangutans (above) are our closest cousins. Their almost human characteristics make them amiable pets, which in turn leads to their downfall as they become the target of poachers. Left and right: While smaller and less aggressive than their African cousins, the Asian elephants still cut a majestic figure. Even as their habitat is being overrun with humans, their numbers in Sumatra are still impressive.*

# A BRILLIANT BIRD LIFE

Indonesia is home to no less than an astonishing 17% of the world's known bird species. Sumatra and Kalimantan share 450 species between them, many common to both islands, such as the various species of the delightful hornbill whose ivory casque has been hunted for centuries. This bird is so beloved by the Dayak people of Kalimantan that they have given it special names; they use the feathers for decoration and base many of their most graceful dances on the bird's movement.

Java and Bali are home to over 300 species, although seeing a bird in Java is something akin to a miracle. As the Javanese are great lovers of caged birds, it is unusual to see one in the wild but the bird markets of the capital cities and regional centres are filled with countless dozens of exotic specimens.

East towards Maluku and Irian Jaya, bird species come to resemble those of Australia with white cockatoos and coloured parrots becoming increasingly common. One of the most spectacular birds in the country is the superb Bird of Paradise whose plumage has been hunted for centuries, both as decorations for the Irian tribal folk as well as for the well-to-do fashion followers in Europe.

*Found in the jungles of Sumatra and Kalimantan, the hornbills (above) are one of the most colourful creatures of the jungle and have been hunted for centuries for their ivory casques. The Bird of Paradise (right) too was hunted, its superb plumage gracing the hats of European gentry for centuries.*

*A bewildering variety of birds can be seen in Indonesia's islands. Above and left: The Nicobar Pigeon and the Argus Pheasant. Far left: The talking Myna bird makes an amusing pet.*
*Facing page, clockwise from top left: Rainbow Parrot; the Papuan Lorikeet from Irian Jaya used for fortune-telling; Golden Oriole; Blue-throated Bee-eater; Lineated Barbet; Magpie Robin; Bennet's Cassowary from Irian Jaya; Crested Wood Partridge from Sumatra. Centre: Oriole.*

# BENEATH THE SEAS

Living in cracks and crevices of the reef, the moray eel (above and right) can grow to a length of over a metre.

With 3.1 million square kilometres of territorial waters, Indonesia has the richest and most diverse marine life in the world. Here in Maluku's whirl of cold and warm currents is the epicentre of the whole Indo-Pacific region, a 19,200-kilometre sweep of marine life. Ten to fifteen per cent of the world's reefs are contained in this incredible archipelago while over 3,000 varieties of fish can be found in its waters. Once a Dutch ichthyologist catalogued 780 species of fish in the reefs off Ambon Harbour, which numbered almost as many as the entire fish population of all the lakes, streams, and seas of Europe. Even the best reefs in the Caribbean can offer only 10 to 20% of the diversity of Indonesia's comparable reefs. With all this richness that represents one million years of evolution, it is hoped it will be preserved and respected for future generations.

A school of Sweetlips graces the sea in one of Indonesia's remote coral reefs (preceding pages). Soldierfish (above) and cuttlefish (left) are some of Indonesia's myriad species. Indonesia, situated right in the midst of the Indo-Pacific region, supports a large proportion of the world's coral reefs and the highest diversity of marine life. The species range from tiny invertebrates to huge pelagic fish and a range of sharks.

*The giant Napolean Wrasse (top left) which grows to over a metre in length and the Blue Parrotfish (top right) are two of the more colourful species that inhabit the reefs. Sea turtles too, can be seen around the archipelago especially the ubiquitous green turtle (above), while the leatherback turtle (left) chooses remote and sheltered beaches to lay its eggs before crawling clumsily back to the sea.*

# MAN AND HIS ANIMALS

In Indonesia, man has put his animals to work. Where machinery is still too expensive or cumbersome to use in the small plots of land that are farmed, man has turned to his animals. The water buffalo is tamed and a compliant helper of man, used to pull the rough ploughs to till the soil. In Sulawesi's Torajaland, valued buffaloes are reared and cosseted by children and treated almost as one of the family. It's rare to see a buffalo without a small keeper around. In parts of Sumatra, golden-haired monkeys are trained to climb trees and pluck the coconuts, tossing them carelessly to the ground for their trainers to collect. Horses from Sumba are employed all over the archipelago to pull the horsecarts known variously as Cidomo, Bendi, or Ben Hur depending on the region. The clip-clopping of their hooves heralds the approach of this picturesque albeit uncomfortable method of travel.

*While the Torajan water buffalo (above) is treated like a valued pet until its sacrifice, the Manado bullocks (below) work every day transporting their owner's produce to market. Bottom: Horse-drawn pony traps are a common sight outside the major cities where rustic pastoral scenes (right) can still be enjoyed.*

*Whether for festivals or everyday use, animal decoration plays a big part in the lives of traditional people. It would be almost unthinkable to hold the Sumba Pasola (facing page, top right) without first dressing the animals in suitable finery. The horsemen of Savu (facing page, top left and bottom) are too, of the same thought. Even the sturdy little ponies that work daily pulling the colourful traps, are dressed before they begin work each day, while the racing bulls of Bali and Madura are dressed lavishly before the races, their horns painted in various colours.*

# They Race Bulls, Don't They?

In Madura they race bulls—both as entertainment for the people and a means of improving the breeding stock of the island. Known as *kerapan sapi*, the races are held in the dry and dusty months of August, September and October after the harvest. With an atmosphere akin to a wild west rodeo, the races are one of the most colourful events on the islands. On race day, the dusty arena can be a village square, an empty field or in the towns, the local open football stadium.

Only the best bulls are used for the races as the stakes are high and the winners garner much prestige. The bulls are fed on a special diet which includes daily doses of chilli, eggs, herbal potions and beer with plenty of soothing music and massage.

Starting at village level, the races progress to regency level before the grand finals which involve the best of the whole island. On the big day, festivities are preceded by processions of the champion bulls dressed in glittering headdresses and bells with their proud owners and their gamelan orchestras—scenes of such pomp and splendour that governors and sometimes, even the President, attends the finals.

*Animal races are not only a great crowd pleaser, they are also used to improve the breeding stock, especially in the Javanese island of Madura (left) while in Sumbawa (above) races help to kill the tedium of ploughing the fields. In Bali (below), well, perhaps the Balinese just like to enjoy themselves in the western reaches of the island.*

## The Serious Art of Cockfighting

Frowned upon by the government and local headmen, cockfighting has almost died out in Indonesia according to official figures. But come afternoon after the work in the fields is done, any *desa* or countryside village in Sumatra, Java, Lombok, Bali or Sulawesi will reveal groups of men sitting about with their prized birds, caressing them, pulling their tail feathers and engaging them in mock battles.

When the real fight is organised, sharp metal spurs known in Bali as *taji* are attached near the cock's upper claw, and used as a sharp extension to wound and kill its opponent. The cocks are more than a pet, they are a possible passport to riches. A cockfight is always accompanied by betting (which is what is frowned upon) and the betting stakes which are usually far higher than the average man can afford, are quite often the road to a family's ruin.

In Bali particularly, cockfighting is an ancient pastime, enjoyed for both ritual and secular occasions. It has long been associated with the ritual blood spilling required to appease any evil spirits that may be lurking nearby. No temple ceremony is complete without the requisite ritual fight held in the temple grounds, and where there's a fight, there's money changing hands and an air charged with excitement.

*While cockfighting is officially banned in Indonesia, allowances are made for Balinese religious ceremonies where blood spilling on temple grounds is part of every major festival. Right: The Balinese keep their cocks in bamboo cages generally placed by the roadside.*

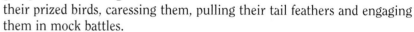

# PART THREE
# PEOPLE, CUSTOMS AND BELIEFS

Strung across Asia's southern extremities like a giant's jewels, the emerald green islands of the Indonesian archipelago are a potpourri of diversely interesting peoples, customs and beliefs. For millennia, it has been the final destination for a series of southern Asian migrations, beginning some 5,000 years ago from Eastern Tibet and China's southern highlands. The gradual movements south down the great river systems of the Mekong, the Yangtze and the Chao Phraya to Indochina, Thailand and finally to Indonesia were marked by two major migrations, that of the Proto-Malays and the Deutero-Malays. The Proto-Malays, represented by Sumatra's Nias islanders and some Dayak tribes in Kalimantan, erected megaliths and practised slash-and-burn agriculture and ancestor worship. Later, the Deutero-Malays arrived, bringing sophisticated cultures with developed religious rites, dance and music and the arts of weaving and pottery.

As these new arrivals made their way to the archipelago, earlier inhabitants retreated inland to remote areas where even today in isolated enclaves, their ancestors follow the old ways. Each successive wave brought new ideas and cultures so disparate that Indonesia has become a nation of nations with a cultural mix more diverse, more intricate, more rich than anywhere else in the world.

The variety of languages is as astonishing as the disparate cultures. Over 300 ethnic groups speaking more than 580 languages and dialects, inhabit this extraordinary island nation. In Irian Jaya alone, the scattered tribal population living in the rugged mountain ranges and deep jungles, speak over 100 distinct languages and innumerable dialects. The binding force that holds such manifold groups together is the national language or Bahasa Indonesia.

While 80% of the country's almost 200 million people follow Islam, Indonesia is not an overtly Muslim nation. Much blending and bending of ideologies, fused together with basic tenets have created unique belief systems like no other country. In the Outer Islands, Christianity has merged with older animistic beliefs, a sometimes satisfying blend where the worst of old customs are put to rest while more tolerable practices are retained. In parts of Java, Islam has mystical overtones and underlying Buddhist and Hindu themes that sit comfortably with the newer religion. Remote parts of Sumatra support an Islam so ascetic as to be almost painful, while the sunny Balinese have evolved a form of Hinduism to an esoteric degree.

While the faces of Indonesia may be sharply different, from the dark skinned grinning countenance of an Irian tribesman to the aesthetic calm of a Javanese gamelan player to the betel-stained mouth of a villager or the absorbed beauty of a Balinese girl making offerings to her God, the Indonesian face has one thing in common without exception—an inner warmth reflected in a winning smile.

*Whether in repose or action the faces of Indonesian dancers reflect an innate elegance like this dancer from the Yogyakarta's royal kraton (left) or these very traditional Balinese dancers (above).*

# MANY PEOPLE, MANY GODS

While the majority of Indonesians follow a form of Islam, it is by no means the only religion. Due to the strong precepts of Indonesia's national ideology, the *Pancasila*, everyone has freedom of religion, although they must worship one supreme god. Multi-deity religions are not accepted and Hinduism has been modified so that even with the pantheon of ancestor figures, deities and spirits, it all rests under the final auspices of Sanghyang Widi Wasa (Supreme God). While officially five religions exist, the many underlying beliefs make for countless regional variations on a main theme.

*Faces around the archipelago reflect the different cultures and beliefs that shape their lives. Facing page, clockwise from top right: A Balinese girl; a young Benuaq Dayak boy from East Kalimantan; a young Sumatran woman from Palembang; a Javanese retainer in Yogyakarta's royal kraton; an elderly Kayan Dayak chief from Kalimantan; a Nias warrior; a Toba Batak elder; a young hawker from Lombok. Centre: A Balinese village girl in traditional dress.*

*Village life encourages a far stronger cultural life than that of the city. These young Balinese college students (top) will have developed a far broader view of the world upon their graduation than that of the Irian Jaya boy (second from top) cocooned in his sarong. The benign betel-stained face of this Sundanese village woman (above) shows that the world outside her immediate sphere holds little interest while the Sumatran woman looking out from her humble abode (left), reflects on a life that could have been happier.*

The men of Irian Jaya love to adorn themselves at any opportunity. Give them a reason and its out with the flowers and soot (mixed with pig fat) and a chance to express their artistic prowess. Beads and baubles are also welcomed and when coloured beads are not available, door keys, bottle caps and even light bulbs can be made into quirky accessories. The Asmat warriors, such as the one on the far top left, like to present a fearsome image while the Dani (right, top right and centre right)) are content with flowers and feathers although the odd pig tusk can be incorporated into the design in times of war (centre left). The Dani, who come from Irian Jaya's Baliem Valley are happier not to wear clothes but merely a penis sheath known somewhat derogatively by the Indonesians as koteka or "tail" (bottom left). These gourd covers come in all shapes and sizes, from small pointy gourds to three feet long spikes that are tied to raise above the shoulder, or squat yellow gourds that make for a convenient carryall.

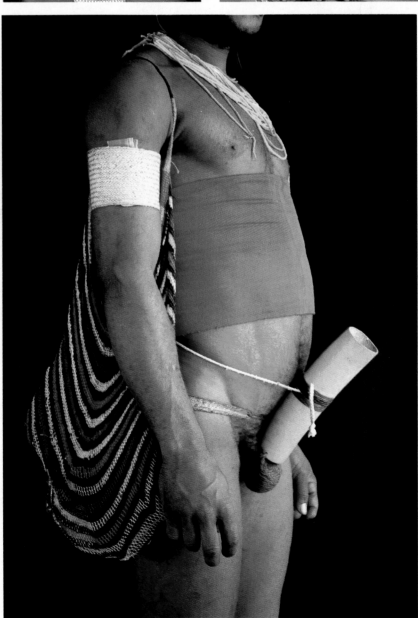

# The Islamic Wali Songo

While Islam was first brought to Indonesia by Arab traders, the Islamisation of Java is believed to have spread after the great rulers of the Hinduised courts were converted to Islam by the Wali Songo or Nine Muslim apostles. These Sufi mystics offered a mystical version of Islam able to compete on equal terms with the cosmic Buddhist and Hindu beliefs at hand.

Numerous legends tell of the Wali's supernatural powers, especially those of the charismatic Sunan Kalijaga, the Demak court's spiritual advisor. His powers were so strong, he is credited with fashioning the four main pillars of Demak's Grand Mosque with his bare hands, pressing wood chips together and fusing them with his supernatural strength. It is said that Sunan Kalijaga helped to spread the word of Islam through shadow puppet (*wayang kulit*) performances and introduced gamelan music to the mosques to attract more believers. To performances of the *Ramayana* and *Mahabharata* epics, he introduced Koranic prayers, thereby subtly introducing Islam to the people in an appealing yet non confrontational manner.

The 15th century saw the conversion of Java's northen coastal kingdoms and the shrines of the nine saints are to be found in the old sultanates of Cirebon, Demak, Jepara, Kudus, Tuban, Gresik, Surabaya, Kediri and Pasaruan, a popular pilgrimage route.

*Demak (bottom left) was the first centre in Java to receive the word of Islam. Islam is Indonesia's strongest religion followed by both men and women (top left) all over the country.*

*Islam reached the Outer Islands like Sumbawa (above and facing page) through trade, while in Java, a more mystical version was introduced by the Sufi mystics. By the early 15th century, small Muslim principalities had developed along the north coast of Java. Older mosques such as this at Kudus along the north coast (top right) reflect Hindu features. On Islamic feast days, mass prayers such as this (far right) are conducted which increase the spiritual strength of the prayer.*

# The Hindu Influence

The Hindu religion has been in existence in Indonesia for more than 1,000 years and its influence is still strongly evident today in dance and theatre. Statuary remains have been found in remote parts of Sumatra and Kalimantan as well as Java and Bali.

Today, the Hindu influence is greatest in Bali where it was brought when the Majapahit courtiers fled their East Java homeland to escape the advent of Islam. Here it has taken root and flowered into a unique form dominated by recognition of Sanghyang Widi Wasa as the Supreme God.

While only small pockets of Hindu believers remain in East Java, the influences are strongly imbued in Javanese culture. Superb temples like Prambanan remain and numerous *candi* are scattered across Java's plains. The age-old rituals of Java's courts or royal *kraton* date back to pre-Islamic times creating an extraordinary melange of both Buddhist and Hindu beliefs. The classical entertainments of both Java and Bali are derived from the great Hindu epic tales of the *Ramayana* and the *Mahabharata*.

Indonesia's national emblem is the mythical Hindu bird, Garuda, Lord Vishnu's winged transport, and both the Indonesian and Javanese languages are peppered with Sanskrit words, even the national philosophy of *Pancasila*.

*The influence of Hinduism once spread across the archipelago, reaching its peak in the 14th century with the great Majapahit Empire which dominated large parts of Indonesia, from Sumatra to points east of Bali. Majapahit's power declined with the advent of Islam and the rise of the Mataram Empire, when the court and courtiers fled to Bali where they established a Hindu kingdom that remains to this day. Top left: Remnants of a Hindu past can still be seen in this Mt. Lawu mountain temple near Surakarta in Java. Top right: The Balinese devised a unique style of art known as the Kamasan-style centred in the Klungkung region. Above and right: Even in Kuta, the most visited part of Bali, traditional ceremonies are held on holy days and even for the opening of hotels.*

# Balinese Offerings

In the refined Balinese world inhabited with spirits and demons, offerings are a daily essential to keep the balance, a harmony between the forces of good and evil. From an early age, girls spend half their life making the folded palm-leaf offerings replete with frangipani blossoms that decorate the island's every step, every temple and every doorway.

While small offerings are suitable for everyday use, temple ceremonies like the annual village Odalan festival require more exotic offerings of fruit and flowers, rice cakes and perhaps a roasted chicken of which the spirit will partake of the essence.

In Bali even the bad spirits, the *butas* and *kalas*, representing the negative side of man and the universe need to be placated but not with pretty playthings. While bad or rotting fruit or pieces of meat will keep them appeased for a short term, what these spirits require most is a sacrifice of blood.

Before an animal is sacrificed whether it be a chicken, pig or a buffalo, prayers are given, mantras recited and offerings made to the living sacrifice, in the hope that it will return to this world as a higher being. For these negative spirits, the size of the sacrifice has a direct bearing on the length of immunity from their evil powers.

*Offerings, offerings, offerings. Every day in Bali all over the island, offerings are made to the gods. Whether in small home shrines (top left), at the beach (left and far left), or in temple festivals (above), offerings play a big part in the lives of the Balinese. These gifts for the gods are intricately fashioned from the inner parts of palm leaves and numerous flowers and the air is always heavy with scent to keep the gods happy. The almost overpoweringly sweet cempaka flower is used extensively and only a whiff of this exotic flower is needed to transport your memory instantly back to Bali.*

# The Buddhist Influence

In Java, Buddhism and Hinduism have merged with so much borrowing and adapting that it is difficult to differentiate the two. Aspects of both religions can be found in each and both are overlaid with Islam.

Bali's dynamic Hindu culture, too, has overtones of Buddhism where ancient moss-covered Buddhist statues lie outside temples. Buddhistic elements of the Hindu dharma derive from a Tantric order of Mahayana or "Greater Vehicle Buddhism" originating from Tibet, Korea, Japan and China.

The largest Buddhist celebration is Waicak day which commemorates the Buddha's enlightenment and birthday together. On the day of the full

moon in May, the grey stone walls of Borobodur and nearby Candi Mendut are flecked with gold as Buddhist monks converge on the ancient sites to pay homage and give prayer. Buddhists come from all Indonesia and abroad to celebrate the holy day.

*Buddhists form a small but devout minority in Indonesia. While centred mainly in Java, in Semarang (below) and around Borobodur and Candi Mendut (above), temples are found in Manado in North Sulawesi too (right). During Waicak, Buddhists converge on Borobodur (facing page) for prayer.*

## A Chinese Presence

Standing on the outskirts of Semarang in Central Java is the town's most visited site. The Gedung Batu Temple or Stone Building Temple commemorates a visit by the Chinese eunuch Admiral Cheng Ho in the early 15th century. An envoy of China's Ming Court, this imperial eunuch made his voyage with an impressive display of power in a fleet of 62 ships and 27,800 men. He made a total of seven voyages to Southeast Asia, Africa and India in an effort to reestablish severed trade routes after China's dynastic wars.

Cheng Ho was a Chinese Muslim, with the consequence that the Gedung Batu Temple is considered sacred by both the Javanese Muslims and the Chinese who attend in large numbers on holy days. His name became associated with many legends and he was later deified as Sam Po Kung—the Three Jewelled Grand Eunuch. Holy shrines honouring his name are found along the northern coasts of Java and Sumatra.

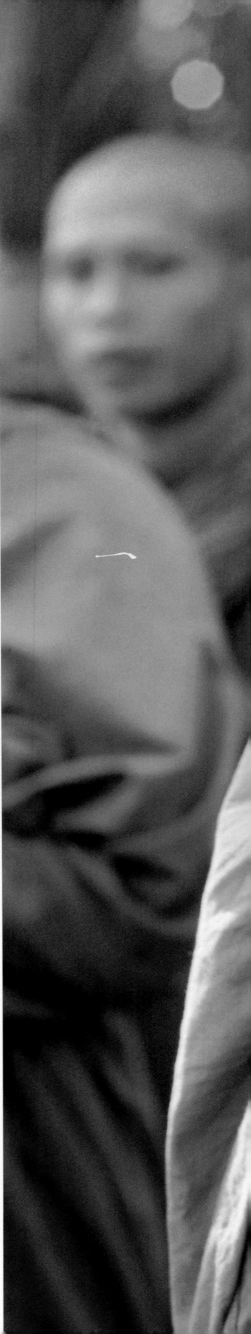

# FESTIVALS—GLIMPSES FROM THE PAST

**M**any of Indonesia's festivals date back to ancient times, age-old rites blended with overlays of newer beliefs and practices so that nothing is quite as it seems and flexibility of beliefs is of the essence. Christian festivals could include a buffalo sacrifice in Toraja or a barefoot midnight Easter procession in Flores or even gamelan-led masses in Yogyakarta. In the royal *kraton* of Java, Muslim festivals like that of the Prophet's birthday will incorporate strong Buddhist-Hindu elements and others dating back to the animistic times of prehistory.

*The ancient Sekaten festival involves much pomp and ceremony and pointed male and rounded female* gunungan *offerings (top and right). At the end of the dignified procession there is a mad scramble for a piece of the offerings (above).*

## Sekaten

While ceremonies occur in Java's palaces on an almost daily basis, the biggest of the annual calendar is Sekaten, a festival originating from the pre-Islamic days of the Majapahit Empire.

The festivities begin a month earlier with a trade fair which in the past would attract itinerant jugglers, musicians and acrobats as well as the traders. Modern music and dance is now a popular feature of the fair.

At 11pm on the first day of Sekaten week, two sacred gamelans are carried from the *kraton* to the royal mosque in a formal procession accompanied by torch-bearing retainers. The gamelans are played alternately throughout the week, filling the grounds with sweet and melodious music. Then on the night preceding Sekaten they are returned to the *kraton* in a midnight procession.

Culmination of the festival is Grebeg Mulud when a bigger and even more stately procession carries offerings in the shape of giant rice mountains from the *kraton* to the royal mosque. Like a scene from a spectacular movie, the richly dressed palace troops march across the town square bearing swords, lances, muskets, bows and arrows and extraordinary headdresses whose origins one can only wonder at.

*Bali's best loved festival, Galungan sees village streets decorated all over the island (below). Women make offerings in their home shrines (below right) and everyone makes a visit to their temple (right) where they receive blessings from the priest. Gamelan music (far right) often accompanies the proceedings in bigger ceremonies.*

# Galungan

Every 210 days (a year in the Balinese calendar) the people of Bali open their doors to welcome their deified ancestors who ascend to earth for the festival known as Galungan, which culminates with the Feast of all Souls, Kuningan, ten days later. All over the island the tinkling sound of gamelan music punctuate the air. Whole villages are decorated, the streets lined with *penjor*, graceful bamboo poles with crafted palm-leaf decorations hanging from their tips.

The origins of the festival hark back to ancient legends now lost in time. It commemorates a legendary battle between opposing armies that once fought in Bali, and celebrates the victory of good over evil and the saving of the world from the forces of darkness.

Deified ancestors are welcomed to earth with offerings, then entertained with performances of dance and music which last far into the night. *Wayang Kulit*, the traditional shadow play, may last till dawn and holy, sacral, trance dances absorb the audience. For the Balinese, Galungan is a time to refresh and reinforce deeply held beliefs, and to renew the faith in the gods.

## Nyale—Festival of the Sea Worms

Along the southern coast of Bali, Lombok and Sumba, an extraordinary event happens one night each year, sometime in February or March. After the priests have made their caculations based on the movements of the moon, prayers have been sent to the requisite gods, the holy men sit back and wait in anticipation of the arrival of the spawning *nyale* or sea worms.

With the appearance of these greenish-black slimy looking creatures comes the time for celebration. In Lombok's Kuta Beach, the appearance of the worms heralds the Bau Nyale festival, a fertility rite and a time for courting and finding a potential mate. In Sumba, it heralds the time to begin Pasola—the island's biggest event of the year. Pasola, the jousting thrusting fight on horseback for hundreds of warriors, was traditionally a time to spill blood, and to let off any tribal steam that had built up over the year. The spilling of blood appeases the spirits and even now, though the spears have been blunted to comply with government regulations, accidents are known to happen and the spirits carry on.

*A high priest (above) monitors the sea for the arrival of the nyale or sea worms. These sea worms live hidden under the rocks near the shore but only surface on one night for procreation purposes. The night when the worms appear is a just cause for great celebration in Bali, Lombok and Sumba. In Lombok, it is the time for courting and looking for a mate. In Sumba, the jousting thrusting Pasola Festival (facing page) begins with the appearance of the sea worms recognised by the high priest. Mounted warriors on horseback are armed with lances (now blunted by government order) and charge at each other fiercely (top and right). Strongly connected with fertility, a Pasola is not considered successful unless blood is spilled.*

# Feast of the Dead

Hidden away in the secluded mountains of South Sulawesi, is Torajaland or Tana Toraja, home to a mysterious traditional people who still follow the old ways. Once the calendars of the Toraja people's lives were filled with festivals and ceremonies, but the advent of the Christian missionaries in the early 20th century caused the cessation of most of them. The biggest festivals today are the elaborate funerals—a high point in the life cycle of every Torajan who follows the old religion.

The funeral is held to transport the soul to the next world, whether to Christian heaven or the traditional *Puya* (Land of Souls) and until the funeral takes place, the body is considered to be still living. Tales are told of Torajan families, who unable to afford the funeral have kept the body in their living room for over fifteen years. To make a funeral complete, sacrifice is required, preferably a buffalo, or in the case of a nobleman, many buffaloes. The ritual area of a major funeral ground resembles a slaughter yard with carcasses of headless pigs and buffalo sprawled, waiting for redistribution to all the attendant families.

After the funeral and the corpse is dispatched amongst great ceremony to a cave high in a rock face, a wooden effigy known as a *tau-tau* is taken to a rock balcony, an intermediary between this world and the next.

*The high point in the life of a Toraja nobleman is the funeral and elaborate preparations are required before any major ceremony. High priests (top right) preside and special buildings (above) are erected. Sacrificial buffaloes are brought into the ceremonial ground (right) where they will be slaughtered in public view.*

*A large funeral requires large numbers of pigs (above) which are later prepared for distribution (left) repaying old obligations. Others prepare meat (far left) for cooking while a scene of slaughter largesse greets the eyes (facing page). While modern funerals are largely Christian in character, it is the Aluk Todolo or old religious ceremonies that are the most interesting. Found in remote parts of Toraja, these ceremonies will include cockfighting and tuak or rice wine in addition to numerous prayers, chants, dances and buffalo sacrifices.*

*The funeral procession (below) entails carrying the heavy timber coffin (left and above) to the grave site and placing it into the prepared hole in the rock face (bottom right).*

*In a funeral involving an aristocrat, a tau-tau effigy (above) will be placed in a hanging balcony carved into a sheer cliff face (facing page). The effigies housed in the cliff balcony wear the clothes of the deceased and are carved to resemble the departed aristocrats. Believed to be the receptacle of the spirit of the dead, the tau-tau are frequently given offerings of cigarettes, tuak (rice wine) and prayers to keep in touch with the departed on his long journey.*

# FROM ANIMIST BEGINNINGS

From ancient times, Indonesians have been deeply attached to the spirit world. Amulets, sacred incantations and invocations are used by village *dukun* described variously as a folk doctor or man of magic, who generally possesses supernatural powers and otherworldly knowledge.

*Dukun* exist in villages all over Indonesia, in Java and Bali particularly, in Kalimantan and the eastern islands. People come seeking solace for any number of complaints—romantic problems, sickness or spiritual matters.

*Even with overlaying belief systems, animistic practices abound in remote areas. These nominally Christian Kenyah Dayaks (left) once hunted heads to keep the spiritual energy strong in their longhouse. Animist priests (top left and centre right) in Sumba keep in touch with the spirits meeting in special annual fiestas (top right), while in Sumbawa, ritual fights (above) keep the spirits high.*

# The Kris—Icon of Power

A symbol of power beloved by many Indonesians and especially the Javanese is the kris, a Malay word for dagger. Much myth and magic surrounds this semi-sacred object that is believed to be imbued with a strength of its own.

Kris are manufactured by the *empu*, a respected and religious craftsman, believed to be imbued with mystical powers. Before making a kris, he will meditate, focusing his energies to produce the most compatible weapon for his client. The *empu* forges a blade from a blended iron ore mixture and the best blade will incorporate nickel-bearing meteorite (to add heavenly power) into the sharp double-sided blade.

*Kris are made by* empu, *highly respected men who must be versed in both the science of metallurgy as well as the mystical realm (above). The* empu *must know about blending metals and in a fine kris it is possible to see the swirling patterns as the black meteoritic metal is mixed with iron.*

The metal is heated before being beaten and folded again and again into a complex series of laminations that will show through on the finished blade in a pattern of stripes along the blade's length. The blade will be either straight or bearing an uneven number of curves, depending on the intended use and the user. Each bend bears a name and a meaning according to mystic Javanese traditions.

While the earliest confirmed date for a kris comes from the 14th century, it is believed that they were in use as far back as the tenth century. Kris are highly valued by their owners who keep their precious weapons "alive" by an annual purification ceremony. Amidst clouds of burning incense, coconut oil and lime juice are used to cleanse the blade, followed with offerings of flowers, food and prayer.

*Embued with magical powers the kris (facing page and left) must be kept "alive" with annual cleansing and rejuvenating ceremonies such as this one at the Surakarta Kraton (above and top right) where amidst clouds of burning incense, the kris are anointed with coconut water before offerings are made.*

# PASAR—LIVING HEART OF A COMMUNITY

*Pasar form the heart of village communities and are often the most colourful and lively place in town. In more remote places goods are laid out on the ground (facing page), while women carry their produce on their heads (above) and even small boys attend stalls (right). Here a woman shops by bicycle (below). Below right: Jamu sellers roam the streets of both towns and villages dispensing health and herbal concoctions with great grace to their clients.*

It is ordinary people that give a country its unique flavour and style and Indonesia is no exception. The *desa* or country villages are the bastions of traditional life, where the old knowledge is nutured and customs preserved.

A strong thread in Indonesia's social fabric, the local *pasar* or market plays a central role in village life and a vital supply line in the bigger towns. Here is more than just a place to buy the vegetables; it is where folk come to exchange information, and to meet with friends. Rural *pasar* are by far the liveliest and most colourful. Traditionally garbed folk from surrounding *kampung* bring their own specialities, whether it be beautifully wrought head-gear or woven cloth, woodcarvings or kitchen wares to exchange for a little much needed cash. Barter has almost completely been replaced by cash, a much sought-after commodity in even the remotest village.

Every day, all over the country, people pile in from the surrounding hinterlands to the *pasar*, bringing fresh produce and home-produced goods and handicrafts to disseminate to the rest of the population.

Just a few years ago, the tribal folk of Irian Jaya's Wamena Valley would pose for pictures in exchange for cash. Because the monetary system was still brand new to their more traditional economies, they preferred red cash (paper notes) little realising that the 100 rupiah (about 5 cents) would buy little in the marketplace. Since then the value of money has entered their system and now the red has been replaced by green or blue of a higher note value.

## The Joys of Jamu

Wandering through the village streets every morning is a woman with a basket of bottles strapped to her back. Invariably she has smooth skin and an elegant walk in spite of the heavy weight of her potions. She is the *jamu* woman selling freshly blended concoctions of herbal medicines that many Indonesians believe will keep them healthy and beautiful.

*Jamu* is commercially produced in big Javanese factories concocting blends of numerous herbs, minerals, grasses, roots, barks, parts of mammals, birds, reptiles and jungle plants. There is *jamu* to keep you young, to improve your skin, your sex life, to stop babies, to make babies, to lose weight and to gain weight. In fact, whatever the problem, there is probably a *jamu* produced that will cure it. Javanese women who take *jamu* regularly can look remarkably attractive even when well into their sixties with several children.

# Indonesia's Folk Transport

Away from the main streets of the big cities with their city minibuses and taxis, the transport of the people is far more colourful. The ubiquitous *becak* or bicycle pedicab is found all over the country and the cheery drivers transport their customers around with great alacrity. The *becak* vary from region to region, some painted with outrageous colourful designs, complete with jingling bells and a high sprung seat for the driver. Even better for the driver, when he has no customers, he can take a seat, sit back and have a snooze in the shade of a big tree and even better for everyone they are noise and pollution free.

Another story altogether are the *bajaj*, noisy little pedicabs fuelled by a smoke-belching motorbike engine. Especially popular in Jakarta's backstreets these little mechanical monsters offer a deafeningly noisy and generally overpriced ride through the city streets.

Prevalent in Bali, the *bemo* is a cheery means of getting around. These tiny little pick-ups can cram a dozen or so passengers into their bench seats and whirl about town and into the country without a moment to lose. Transport to even reasonable distances cost only a few cents.

*Bendi* or colourful horse-drawn carts can be found in rural areas all over the country. In the royal town of Yogyakarta, the *bendi* takes a different, more sedate form and is known as an *andong*. In Sumbawa, they are known whimsically as "benhurs" after the chariots ridden by the Roman warrior. In Lombok the country roads are littered with *cidomo*.

*Indonesia's folk transport consists primarily of the ubiquitous* becak *(right), while the horse-drawn cart (top left, facing page top, centre and bottom) can be seen in towns across the country. Sumatra's rough country tracks favour hardy buses (above). Folk transport in Indonesia is generally colourful. What the operators lack in financial terms they make up for in imagery. Becak and trucks are decorated with colourful Indonesian scenes of mountains and lakes and sometimes luridly colourful pictures of girls. Sumatran buses are a riot of colour, chrome trim supplementing a rainbow riot of colour scheme, the other side of the coin to the refined and traditional art and culture. In stately Yogyakarta, the andong or horse-and-cart are trimmed with royal yellow, the colour of the sultans.*

# URBAN LANDSCAPES

As Indonesia's industrial revolution gathers momentum, the demography of the country changes, as more people flock to the cities in search of work and opportunities for a better life. The movement is particulaly strong in Java's big cities, which in 1990, held 69% of Indonesia's total urban population of around 55 million. The projection for the urban population for the year 2000 is 76 million or 36% of the population.

The capitals of Jakarta, Bandung and Surabaya are the biggest, fastest growing in the country and experts are already referring to Jabotabek, encompassing the urban centres of Jakarta, Bekasi, Bogor and Tangerang. Now analysts predict that eventually the corridor from Jakarta to Bandung will be one great urban conglomeration.

*Life in the city. Both day and night, Jakarta's busy streets (top left and right) form a startling contrast to the quiet rural areas while pedicaps such as this (above centre) form a noisy and expensive way of getting around. A boy sells newspapers (top centre) after school hours to help make ends meet. These truck drivers enjoy a well-earned rest in the shade of their truck (above).*

## Jakarta—The Mother City

Jakarta, or Ibu Kota ("mother city"), is the biggest, busiest city in Indonesia where something approximating 70% of the nation's wealth is generated. With a population estimated at anywhere between nine and twelve million, Jakarta is already a big city, the eighth largest in the world and growing fast.

But as in any big city the contrasts are there—the very rich co-existing alongside the very poor, the heights of luxury with the depths of squalor. Many improvement programs have been initiated in Jakarta over the last decade and abundant foreign investment is transforming the massive *kampung* or village beyond recognition.

Sophisticated world-class hotels lure the rich. Handphone-wielding businessmen relax at Hard Rock Cafe or the newest American-style nightclubs like Fashion Cafe and Planet Hollywood. Fast-food franchises like McDonalds and KFC lure the young. Glitzy new shopping malls sell international designer brand names at highly inflated prices while new arrivals from the *desa* look on in awe.

But while the rich enjoy the bright lights and all the attractions and diversions money has to offer, Jakarta has countless other tales to tell. This city of 12 million people continues to attract the hopeful as more and more folk leave the countryside in the great urban migration. The penurious and hopeful come and try their luck. Roadside hawkers who risk their lives dodging traffic each day as they sell papers, statues or even cold water to passing motorists can make several thousand rupees a day—a small fortune for a penniless farm worker.

Even now despite the fast-growing rash of glittering new office towers and apartment blocks that appear along the crowded main thoroughfares, Jakarta is a giant *kampung* where literally hundreds of villages have amalgamated to make an immense metropolis.

# PART FOUR

# ART AND ARCHITECTURE

Like clues dropped by some mischievous giant, mysterious monuments are scattered liberally across Indonesia's plains and jungles. Hidden in the depths of Sumatra's deep forests are the enigmatic faces of ancient Hindu monuments carved in stone. And too, deep in the heart of Indonesian Borneo, up remote almost uncharted rivers are stone images from a distant past.

In Sulawesi's hidden Bada Valley, twelve-foot megaliths dot an almost deserted valley—their smooth faces and vaguely phallic outlines reveal no hints as to their long forgotten origins. Odd stones bear indecipherable carvings from another age. In the islands of Nias, in Sumba and in Sumatra, tribal groups once worshipped the stone image of other less forgotten gods.

In Java, the monuments are more substantial, their history better recorded. Standing on the uplands of East Java, overlooking Surabaya, temples and stone figures of the Singosari Kingdom still stand vigil over their former domain.

While thousands of lesser *candi* and carvings dot the plains of Central Java, the great monuments of Borobodur and Prambanan bear tribute to the great skill of the stone carvers. Passed down from generation to generation these skills are still so highly honed that it is difficult for even an expert to differentiate between an ancient carving and one recently made.

The artistry of the stone carvers is only one facet of Indonesia's multi-talented artisans. The people seem to be born with natural skills already infused into their very being. Art cannot be separated from life and in Bali, there is no word for art. Traditionally, the work of each woodcarver, each dancer, each painter or puppeteer, would be made as an offering to his god. Money or even acknowledgement of his skills plays no part in the transaction.

The artisans' skills are reflected in villages across the country where women and men fashion crafts that would justify prominence in an exclusive gallery. The purity of form of simple grass-fired clay pots reflect styles that have been perfected over the centuries, while using the most basic of techniques. Baskets, hats of all dimensions, mats, woodcarvings and even brooms bear the stamp of great dexterity.

Weaving and textiles are diverse to the point of unbelievability. While batik is known far and wide, and the *ikat* artistry of Sumba has long held prominence amongst collectors, regional variations in weaving techniques and styles, such as the silk *ikat* of the Bugis, the *hulos* of the Batak, the *songket* of Palembang, or the filigreed *tapis* of Lampung await discovery.

Dance is just one more facet of Indonesia's creative heritage that is expressed throughout the country. Whether it is a warrior's dance from a Kalimantan longhouse or a village harvest celebration in Lombok, dances are executed finely and with great style. The fight of good against evil is a frequently recurring theme that appears again and again, especially in many of the classical dances of both Bali and Java. Interpretations of the Hindu epics of the *Ramanaya* and the *Mahabharata*, repeat the theme in a motif that never tires.

*Art and architecture is aptly reflected in the sublime carving of Borobodur (above) while these masked Lombok dancers (left) continue the traditions of their forefathers.*

# MEGALITHIC MONUMENTS

In parts of Indonesia, the last remnants of a megalithic age are still alive even as the industrial and electronic eras are being ushered in. While some megalithic cultures are still in practice, vestiges of others can be found all over the archipelago. The strange stone statues of Sulawesi's Bada Valley have long since lost links with their origins and are a mystery to all, while the people of Torajaland use huge stone blocks in the *rante* or ceremonial ground for their funeral rituals. Others like the Batak of North Sumatra know their origins well but the old traditions are losing ground. The people of Nias and Sumba have impressive megaliths that still play a part in their culture. Sumba's megalithic tombs can be found right in the village centre. These tombs of thick stone slabs are surprisingly similar to those of Sumatra's Toba Batak.

*Some Indonesian megalithic cultures are still alive as shown by this Nias initiation cermony (above). The origin of other megaliths, like those of the Bada Valley (top left) are long forgotten. Sumba villages (top right) too have megalithic themes.*
*Right: The Batak villages of Samosir Island are littered with numerous solid heavy tombs and a colourful oral history to accompany them. Facing page: West Sumba is known for its fine megalithic tombs that often depict heavy figures associated with royalty.*

# MEDITATION IN STONE

**D**escribed as the greatest single Buddhist monument in the world, Borobodur is part of a complex of *candi* (temples) and shrines that dot Central Java's Kedu Plain. This replica of the cosmic Mt. Meru was the cosmological and spiritual centre of the Sailendra Kingdom built during the eighth and ninth centuries, about three hundred years before Angkor Wat.

After a brief period of glory, the Sailendra Empire quickly declined in the tenth century as power shifted to East Java. Earthquakes and volcanic activity caused Borobodur to disappear beneath a mound of volcanic rubble for almost a millennium. It was rediscovered centuries later by T.S. Raffles in 1814 during his brief reign as Governor of Java. He had heard tales of the "stone knights on the mountain" and upon investigation by his engineer H.C. Cornelis, Borobodur was revealed.

A series of restorations had little long-lasting effect until the UNESCO funded renovation program dismantled it in its entirety in 1973. Around 1,300,000 blocks of stone were documented, cleaned, chemically treated and reassembled over a new concrete foundation, at a cost of US$23 million. The newly completed monument was opened in 1983 and is guarded and protected to preserve this marvellous heritage for future generations.

*C*oloured with the light of evening, the stone figures of Borobodur turn to gold (preceding pages). From the air, the clean-cut layout of Borobodur is revealed in its simplicity (above) and from a distance the monument appears quite humble (below). A close-up (facing page) reveals the skill of the ancient carvers.

*T*he Hindu builders of Candi Plaosan (below) and Loro Jonggrang (above) made monuments whose elegance would last for eternity.

## The Prambanan Plain

Scattered across the Prambanan Plain are relics of more than fifty Hindu temples that once comprised the 10th century Mataram Kingdom. Its lofty spires standing out above the rest, the graceful Loro Jonggrang Temple ("Slender Maiden"), also known as Prambanan Temple, is the most impressive of all the Hindu temples here. Constructed between A.D. 900 and 930 it was built to commemorate the Sanjaya Kingdom's victory over the Sailendras, but it was deserted just a few years later.

The symmetry and graceful proportions of the temple set it apart from the rest as it stands amidst the sculptured rubble of the still incomplete surrounding *candi*. The carefully modelled details reveal scenes from the *Ramayana*, and portray a good impression of Javanese daily life in the 10th century. While preparations for its restoration were begun in 1918, work only started in 1937 and it was not until 1953 that the main towers were completed.

# THE KRATON—ABODES OF ROYALTY

Based upon a miniature model of the cosmos, the Javanese *kraton*, or abode of royalty, is more than a residence—it is a political power centre as well as spiritual. The sultan and his intimate subjects live encased behind the thick protective walls. Dignified batik sarong-clad retainers, their kris neatly tucked into their waistband, stand by on hand in the almost deserted courtyards. Outside the walls, in the crowded surrounding *kampung*, live the *kraton* familes, drawn upon for the sultan's well-being and needs—the craftsmen who supply material needs and the musicians and dancers who perform at the royal court.

Of all Java's *kraton*, Yogyakarta's Ngayogyakarta-Hadiningrat is the epitome of everything gracious about Javanese life. Behind the white stone walls, a serene and refined world is revealed, a place of order where every gateway, every plant has symbolic meaning. Built along a north-south axis, the *kraton* points towards Mt. Merapi, the source of spiritual power and residence of the gods. Its walls conceal smaller courtyards and reception areas within. Open-sided pavilions offer a respite from the hot sun.

*Refined and peaceful, Surakarta's Kraton Mangkunegaran (below) sits behind solid protective walls (above). The Mangunegoro royal family (facing page, top) live within the* kraton *confines.*

Cirebon on Java's north coast has four kraton within its city boundaries. With Indonesia's independence came the end of the good life for many Javanese royal residences. But traditions live on and the courtliness and grace of the kraton epitomises the essence of the Javanese royalty. Here, the foyers of Kraton Kasepuhan in Cirebon favour European-style decor (bottom) and retains a carriage (below) of extraordinary proportions and mystical powers, depicting a blend of Garuda, dragon and elephant.

*I*ndonesia's most famous palace, Kraton Ngayogyakarta-Hadiningrat in Yogyakarta is inhabited by the gracious Sultan and his wife (left) who live in a state of regal splendour (below). After the ornate royal carriages are renewed and blessed in a ceremony each year, they are guarded by a place retainer (bottom) while people file past to pay their respects.

*T*he inner walls of the kraton are decorated with finery from Europe (facing page). Gilt-framed mirrors hang from the walls and cast-bronze statuettes hold electric lamps. In the distance, there is always the shadow of abdi dalem, the name given to palace retainers who devote their life to the safeguard of the sultan, existing on a small stipend. Their batik sarong feature designs unique to the court, each denoting the rank of the wearer.

# INDONESIA'S EXTRAORDINARY ENDEMIC ARCHITECTURE

**F**ound in isolated pockets in Sumatra, Kalimantan, Sulawesi, Nias, Irian Jaya, Bali and Sumba are villages whose extraordinary architecture defies description. Villages are aligned according to *adat* or customary law. In Torajaland, for example, the house will always face north while in Bali, each compound is set out according to a tried and tested pattern.

High roofs, thick slab timbers for the foundations and cramped living spaces seem to be the salient features of many of Indonesia's indigenous homes. Striking similarities can be seen between the Batak and Toraja houses and those in southern Nias. Families of eight or ten would occupy a floor space of no more than nine square metres. Even more remarkable are some of the communal houses of the larger Karo Batak houses where eight families share a space not bigger than an average family home in the city. Being unencumbered with too many possessions, it is possible to accommodate up to fifty or even more into one space.

Some of the most beautiful examples of endemic architecture are to be found in West Sumatra where the curving roofs of the Minangkabau villages rise to distinctive pointed spires, echoing the curve of a buffalo's horns. These matrilineal people build on to the original house as the family grows or as a woman marries.

*T*he outlying islands are distinguished by individual architectural styles such as these Dani huts in the Baliem Valley (above) and the Sumba meeting-house (above top). Right and below: The Minangkabau people of West Sumatra live in magnificent spired-roof houses said to echo the horns of the buffalo. Facing page: A Minangkabau woman with a headdress also resembling buffalo horns.

In Sumba, traditional villages conform to a particular pattern as well as the houses within. Their high peaks and thatched roofs are built around a fireplace and one of their most appealing features is the two-entrance system. While men enter through the front door, women use the back entrance.

The Dani people of Irian Jaya's Wamena Valley live in small grass huts that look rather like overgrown mushrooms. The thick grass walls and roof protect against the cold of the higher mountain regions.

*The Toraja people of South Sulawesi live in carved and decorated houses with extraordinary saddle-backed roofs (above and right). In front of each house, carved and decorated rice barns (left) are used to store the rice.*

*While Bali's upmarket hotels most closely follow traditional endemic architecture, this ancient rice barn (above left) is a relic from the past. Another anachronism is Kampung Naga in West Java (above right) whose inhabitants staunchly refuse the trappings of the 20th century. While the Batak of North Sumatra are less idealistic, many choose to continue using traditional adornments (facing page).*

# THE DUTCH INFLUENCE

For over three hundred years, the Dutch held their prominent position in Indonesia. They built their colony with suitably imposing administrative buildings and fine residences. The stuccoed brick exteriors were sturdy and of durable construction. As the Dutch believed that bad air was responsible for disease, the windows tended to be small, more suited to cold northern climes than the heat of the tropics.

While many Dutch buildings were razed after *Merdeka* (Independence), especially in Jakarta, many of the most impressive were left standing. Solid and durable, these buildings still stand today in the major towns, taken over as banks and government offices, presidential palaces in Jakarta and Bogor and as residences for many Indonesian families.

*With over three hundred years in Indonesia, it is no surprise that the Dutch left some architectural legacy although this church in Semerang (top) looks more Greek than Dutch. The Bogor Presidential Palace offers a pleasing symmetry (centre) while the imposing Gedung Sate (above) is one of Bandung's most impressive and well-known buildings.*

## Bandung's Tropical Deco Architecture

Hotels shaped like ocean liners with big round porthole windows and Egyptian details are all features of tropical art deco architecture that was so popular in the 1930s. At the time of the new architectural rage, Bandung was being considered as Indonesia's new colonial capital. Money was plentiful and the planters were doing well with tea, coffee, quinine and other crops.

Prominent architects were brought in from Holland and a sense of whimsy was in the air. Today Bandung has an extraordinary collection of over 600 registered tropical art deco buildings on a par with Napier in New Zealand and Miami in the United States.

One of the best examples is the still original Savoy Homann Hotel in Jalan Asia Afrika. With its curving walls and steamship motif created by Wolf Schoemaker, it has been faithfully restored, without losing any of its art deco charm. High upon a hill overlooking the city is another interesting building of this style, the Villa Isola, a house with a romantic past now converted to accommodate generations of student-teachers.

Others include the inappropriately named Gedung Sate or Sate Building, one of the town's most imposing public buildings, built along formal geometric lines with art deco details. Today the very active Bandung Heritage Society is working hard to preserve Bandung's art deco heritage. The Society has raised civic pride in the city and now even new buildings are echoing the elegant style of the 30s.

# Kota Batavia
# —Jakarta's Old Dutch Capital

Designed as a smaller version of Amsterdam, Batavia, the old Dutch capital of Java was built on the razed ruins of Jayakarta located in the northern part of today's Jakarta. The new settlement was established in 1828 by Jan Pieterszoon Coen, envoy of the VOC. With grandiose plans he envisioned it as the administrative and military hub of all the Dutch possessions, which stretched from Southern Africa across to East Indonesia with small outposts in Japan and Taiwan.

Built on flat marshy lowlands, Coen drained the land using a system of five canals. His plan included expansion of the original Batavia Fort to a walled city. Drawbridges crossing the canals allowed access of ships to the docks and trading centres where giant warehouses or godowns stored the precious spices and pepper that would bring them so much wealth. Sturdy barracks were built for the soldiers and civic and municipal buildings faced the town square (now Fatahillah Square), the site of the administrative centre for a vast mercantile empire.

By the turn of the 19th century, Batavia had declined along with the fortunes of the VOC. On his appointment as Governor-General in 1808, H.W. Daendels demolished the old fort around the harbour, moving the city centre to a new location where the wide tree-lined boulevards and gracious houses set the foundations for modern Jakarta.

The Kota district was ignored. Recently, a resurgence of interest in Kota Batavia has led to renovations of some of the old buildings, while new hotels and cafes have sprung up, bringing a spark of life to this interesting old section of town.

*Bandung's 30s' whimsical tropical art deco architecture has set it apart from other Indonesian cities. The graceful lines of the Savoy Homann Hotel (bottom right), the Villa Isola (below left) and the West Java Bank (below) portray tropical art deco at its best. Top left: Fatahillah Square was once the centre of the VOC Empire and this salon (left), probably once housed an important merchant family.*

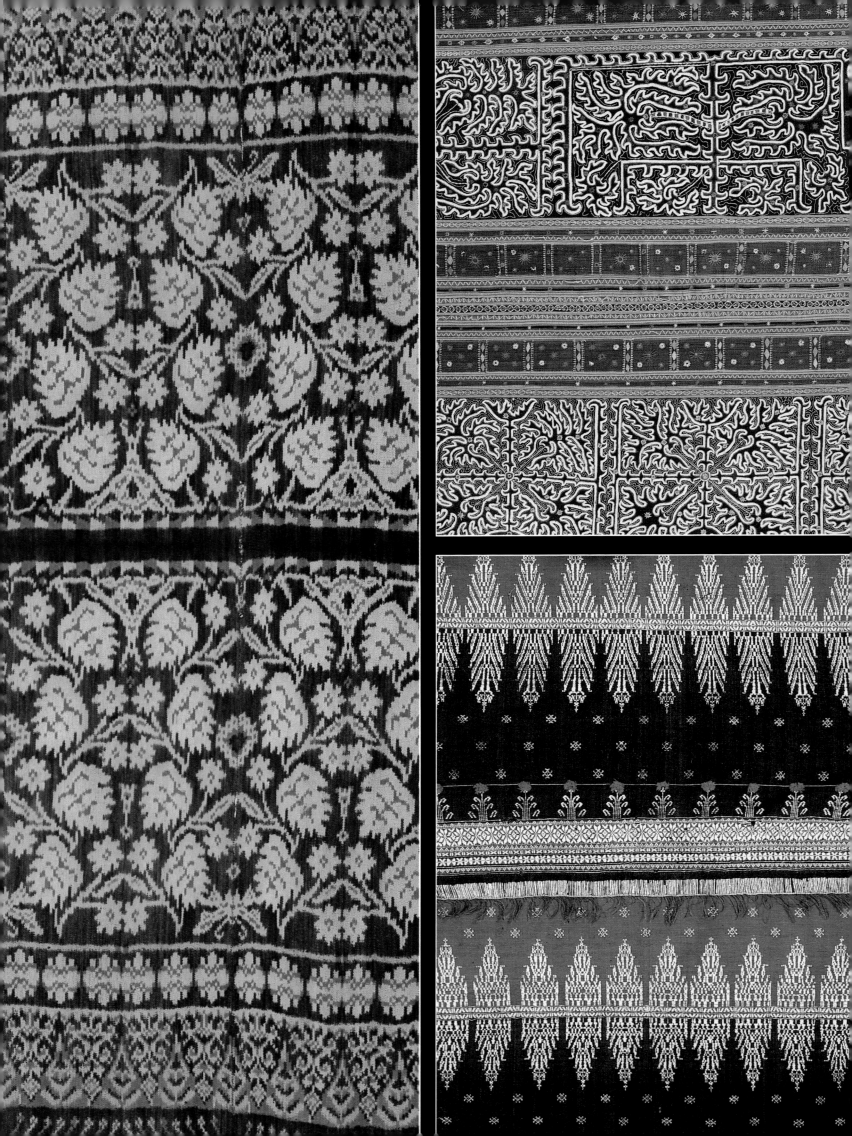

# TEXTILES—WOVEN DREAMS

Indonesia has perhaps a more diverse collection of traditional textiles than any other country in the world. For centuries, weaving has played an important part in village life where a woman's dreams and aspirations as well as status, rank and social standing can be woven into a piece of handloomed cloth.

Any form of weaving known can be seen in a country where women using traditional handlooms produce textiles for daily use and ceremonial occasions. Prints, weaves, *ikat*, double *ikat*, silk, *songket* weaving with gold or silver thread are made as well as other plaids. In Bali, exuberant textiles, both old and new are immeasurably varied.

*Woven dreams. Often a master weaver will dream of a new motif which her advanced skills will enable her to translate into a fine piece of woven cloth. The fine art of* ikat *or tie-dye is widespread from Sumatra to Bali and Lombok, although the form reaches its peak in the eastern islands of Sumba (above and top) and Timor (facing page, left). Many other styles are also produced throughout the islands like this Sumatra weave (facing page, bottom right). Lampung textiles (right and facing page top right) are well regarded.*

*This Balinese songket textile (above) makes a glittering costume for weddings and other ceremonial occasions. Songket, which sometimes incorporates gold or silver thread into the design, is produced all across the western Indonesian islands.*

## Bali's Sacred Geringsing Cloth

Adored by serious textile collectors for its intricacy and sophisticated techniques, Bali's *geringsing* is a masterpiece of the weaving craft. The cloth is made by the Bali Aga, Bali's original inhabitants, in a handful of remote villages in east Bali.

Believed to hold magic properties, the textile is used to protect the wearer from serious illness. Traditionally, it is used in formal festivals and rites of passage ceremonies like tooth filing and wedding ceremonies and to cover the dead before burial.

*Geringsing* is woven by the double *ikat* method whereby both weft (crosswise) and warp (lengthwise) threads are tied and dyed into complex motifs before weaving. After weaving on a simple handloom, the threads must match up to form an integrated pattern.

The muted colours of dark reds, creams and browns are derived from natural vegetable dyes collected from the forest. With the work of gathering the plants, extracting the dyes, spinning and binding the thread, and the actual weaving itself, interspersed with farm work and looking after the house, it could take up to ten years to make one piece of this highly valued textile.

Sadly the art of making *geringsing* is dying out and only a few skilled weavers in the Bali Aga villages are still able to produce a quality piece.

*Java's best batik is* tulis *or hand drawn either in factories (below) or in homes. Mixed stamp and hand drawn batik is produced in factories alone (left). The three distinctively different Javanese batik styles (right, bottom and facing page) each display regional variations.*

# Batik—Symbol of a People

Batik cloth worn daily by millions of Indonesians is very much a symbol of the country. Still very much alive in Java is the production of the cloth, an intricate process involving the application of hot liquid wax resist to cloth, then dyeing it. The unblocked areas take up the dye. The process is repeated up to seven times on one piece, producing a beautifully finished textile.

When application is made using a copper pen known as a *canting,* it is called *batik tulis* or hand-drawn batik and one piece can take months to complete. Other methods involve the use of copper stamps which are dipped in the wax, then placed carefully to make the pattern.

There are literally dozens of batik centres in Java, each area with its own specific style. In the royal court cities of Yogyakarta and Surakarta, colours and designs are restrained and quiet— with heavy use of indigo blues, tans and cream—the designs mostly abstract renditions due to the Islamic prohibition of portraying living things. Along the north coast where heavy outside influences have come along with trade, motifs are more exuberant, using pretty floral motifs and colours are brighter with reds and yellows predominating, yet no less well executed.

Commercially made batik is gaining in popularity as the market continues to demand affordable everyday wear. At the other end of the market is the superb hand-painted silk batik which is far more a luxury item demanded by the rich.

# INDONESIA'S VERSATILE CRAFTS

$S$till steeped in tradition, the artisans of Indonesia produce an amazing array of crafts in the time-tested ways of centuries past. Youngsters learn by the simple method of watching their elders, picking up the intricacies as they go along until they begin to practise for themselves.

Baskets cover a multitude of purpose. Made from rattan, or grasses and different palm fibres, there are baskets for storage, for carrying padi, for winnowing, for transporting goods and for keeping precious items. The best baskets are made from rattan, a durable and long-lasting material that gradually acquires a beautiful golden brown patina from constant use.

In many parts of the country, especially in Kalimantan, mats are used constantly as portable sleeping gear and floor coverings. The beautifully woven rattan mats of Kalimantan's Punan people are the most striking and probably the most intricate in the world.

The best of the crafts are made for personal use, for utensils and household items. Materials are drawn from the host of natural substances at hand. The jungle provides rattan and bamboo and vines to bind, while the coconut tree provides wood, fibres and the smooth hard shell of the fruit which is so amenable to carving. Palm leaves and pandanus become baskets and fine mats.

From the earth comes the clay that is fashioned into quirky figures and beautifully formed water pots and cooking utensils and the earthy red terracotta tiles that adorn the village roofs.

*Lombok is well known for its crafts such as these baskets (above), newer ceramic sculptures (right) and the pure lines of its traditional pottery (centre and bottom right), while the Balinese produce crafts of all descriptions, both modern and traditional, like this stone carver of Bali (bottom left).*

*Balinese crafts incorporate woodcarvers, especially around Mas, near Ubud, where some of the best masks (right) are created. The Balinese are known as perhaps the most creative of all the Indonesians. All over the island, there is a diversity of creative talents and marvellous colourful things to buy that defies imagination. Sumatra too has its share of superb crafts as this Batak jewellery (left) and Palembang betel-nut set (below) will attest.*

# DANCE AND DRAMA

**D**ance comes in myriad forms. In Indonesia, dance is closely associated with rituals, with celebrations of rites of passage, agricultural events of planting and harvests and major events in the village history. The dance incorporates features of storytelling and trance, especially Bali's famous trance dances and Java's *kuda lumping*, a hobbyhorse dance where participants take on the mannerisms of a horse.

While most folk dances are energetic and vibrant, requiring little formal training, the classical dances of Bali and Java are just the opposite. The dances derive mostly from the great Hindu epics of the *Ramayana* and the *Mahabharata* featuring the timeless tales of the struggle of good against evil. They have played an important part in instilling traditional Javanese values, especially through the medium of dance and the shadow puppet or *wayang kulit*.

Children in both Bali and Java begin classical dance training at an early age, around six years old. Their supple fingers learn to form numerous gestures, each imbued with meaning.

*The restrained grace of classical Yogyakarta and Surakarta dancers (facing page and centre right) contrasts dramatically with the birdlike hand gestures of the Benuaq Dayak warrior dance (above) and the flamboyant masculinity of the Kenyah warrior's dance (bottom left).*

## Wayang Kulit —The Village Television

There is still some doubt about where the shadow puppets came from but it is generally agreed that the *wayang kulit* had its origins in India, before spreading to Southeast Asia where it has reached the pinnacle of the art in Java and Bali.

While the main stories portrayed versions of the *Ramayana* and *Mahabharata* epics, the *wayang* was later used throughout Java rather much like television is today, to disseminate information to the people. During the Islamisation of Java, the word of Islam was brought to the people and later the very effective family planning message to rural Java and Bali. Later too it was used to spread political messages across the islands.

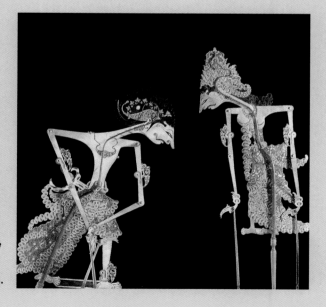

*These dancers from an island off Sumba (top right) are performing a newly resurrected old dance form for the first time while the kuda lumping (centre top left) causes dancers to fall into deep trance, adopting horse-like behaviour.*
*Following pages: Bali's whimsical Barong is a sacred creature that lives in the temple, only being brought to life for important temple festivals and celebrations.*

## Balinese Dance—A Gift for the Gods

Balinese dance comes in myriad forms—a tribute to the gods for the enjoyment of the community. Those ethereal creatures that take the stage are transformed with paint, costume and prayer from their daily lives as rice farmers or fishermen, woodcarvers or painters.

Over 50 dances are performed in Bali including mask dances, *legong*, *baris*, *jauk* and *janger*, not to mention the very dramatic trance dances. Heavily stylised, each gesture is learned and remembered until it becomes second nature to the dancer, but the spiritual energy that infuses each performer makes it seem like a first performance.

Among Bali's most popular dances is the Legong Kraton or Palace Legong, formerly patronised by rajas within the palace grounds. It is best performed by pre-pubescent girls. Baris is a traditional war dance glorifying the warrior. Whether performed singly or in a group, it is a dynamic dance accompanied by the gamelan gong attuned to the changing movements of the dancer. Known for its lively chanting of the *chak-a-chak* sounds of the chorus, the *kecak* or monkey dance enacts scenes from the ancient *Ramayana* epic. The chorus of up to 150 men clothed in black and white sarong chant and sway while the action unfolds centre stage.

*Barong dances are now performed for tourists at many places in Batubulan (left) as well as in traditional temple festivals. The most charming of dances, the* legong *(above) has entranced generations of visitors to Bali as has the* kecak *or monkey dance (right), here performed for a traditional ceremony at the beach. The majestic Baris Gede (top) is a warrior dance whose dances come from communities around Kintamani.*

## The Gamelan Orchestra

Described as sounds of moonlight by American musicologist Colin McPhee who visited Bali and Java in the 1930s, the gamelan orchestras of Bali and Java are assemblages of Indonesia's most evocative and distinctive sounds.

Accompanying every *wayang* performance, every classical dance, used to herald Madura's bull races, to add an air of serenity in sophisticated hotel lobbies and as a vital ingredient of any *kraton* ceremony or Balinese dance or temple ritual, the sounds of gamelan orchestra are an integral part of the culture.

While the ensemble varies according to the situation, the main feature is always a large bronze gong—an ancient Javanese tradition. Bronze xylophones, too, are essential to the sound.

Each gamelan has its own identity and sound; being manufactured by hand no two sound quite alike. Instruments are tuned to intricate and overlapping scales that produce an ethereal sound that constantly teases the senses. While a gamelan orchestra uses no written music, its complexity requires intricate timing regulated by the drummer.

# ART CENTRES OF BALI AND YOGYAKARTA

*While great paintings are created in Bali, the "art by the metre" style of painting (below and centre right) is a lucrative business, and is very popular with tourists.*

**W**hile talented painters are busily at work in all corners of Indonesia, the main art centres are concentrated in Bali and Yogyakarta where the atmosphere seems to be imbued with creative energy. International collectors are buying, and the art scene is vibrant.

The 30s saw a revitalisation of Bali's art scene when the exotic island attracted Western painters to its shores, who showed talented local painters new ideas and techniques away from the more classical traditional styles of the past.

As in Bali, the artistic centre of Yogyakarta with its traditions of *wayang*, batik painting and surreal figures provide a fertile spawning ground for new talent. The Yogyakarta Art School is helping to foster the new talents.

Given the exuberance of the Balinese and other Indonesians, styles will change and evolve as whole new schools of young modern painters emerge, eager to express themselves.

*Bali's extraordinarily fertile and creative atmosphere draws artists from all over Indonesia and abroad. Painters such as Rudolf Bonnet (whose paintings are on the facing page and top left) arrived in the 30s while Soedarsono (painting at left) is a more modern addition. Affandi (with his famous self-portrait, far left), perhaps Indonesia's most well-known painter spent his most creative years in Yogyakarta and not in Bali at all.*

NEW
GUINEA

Wamena
Baliem Valley
Jayapura
Jayawijaya
Baliem River
Digul River
Mamberano River
Puncak Jaya
Paniai Lakes
Merauke

IRIAN JAYA

Biak
Yapan
Aru Islands

Sorong

PACIFIC OCEAN

Arafura Sea

Tanimbars

Babar

Banda Islands
Ceram
Ambon
Banda Sea
Halmahera
MALUKU
(Moluccas)
Ternate
Tidore
Bacan
Sula Islands
Buru

I      N      D      O      N      E      S      I      A

Wetar
Alor
Dili
Timor
Kupang

Timor Sea

AUSTRALIA

Manado

PHILIPPINES

Sulu Sea

Mt.Keli
Mutu
Adonara
Lembata
Komodo
Rinca
Flores
Savu
Sumba
Sumbawa

SULAWESI
Kantepao

Lake Poso

Ujung
Pandang

Makassar Straits

Flores Sea

NUSA TENGGARA

Lombok

LESSER SUNDAS

SOUTH CHINA SEA

Samarinda

Balikpapan

Barito River

Mahakam River

MALAYSIA
(EAST)

BRUNEI

BORNEO
(KALIMANTAN)

Banjarmasin

Kapuas River

Tanjung Puting
Nature Reserve

Java Sea

Gunung
Agung
BALI
Denpasar
Mt.Bromo
Mt.Semeru
Madura
Surabaya
Surakarta
(Solo)
Prambanan
JAVA
Mt.Merapi
Semarang
Borobudur
Yogyakarta
Cirebon

Pontianak

Natuna Islands

THAILAND

MALAYSIA
(WEST)

SINGAPORE

Riau Archipelago

Gulf of Thailand

Jambi

Palembang

Bengkulu

SUMATRA

Padang

Bukittinggi

Lake Toba

Medan

Siboga

Nias

Sabang
Banda Aceh

Mentawai Islands

JAKARTA
Batavia
Bogor
Bandung

Telukbetung
Krakatau
Ujung Kulon
National Park

Sunda Straits

INDIAN OCEAN

# INDONESIA
## PORTRAITS FROM AN ARCHIPELAGO

*Created by the Sailendra Dynasty, in the 9th century, Borobodur was mysteriously deserted soon after, left to be buried under volcanic rubble and detritus for centuries until it was rediscovered by British Thomas Stamford Raffles centuries later.*

With its superb topography of volcanoes and cultivated rice fields, Java was long described by the Dutch as the "Garden of the East" or the "Paradise of the East", a title that could still be applied today (facing page). Ternate (above) and its twin island Tidore both played an important part in the days of the Spice Trade. After early tradings with the Portuguese and Spanish, the Tidore Sultan chose to deal with the Dutch as a lesser evil.

*These beautiful 19th century illustrations of Sumatran wildlife are more works of art than graphic depictions of the animals (above). Featured are a wild boar (top left), macaques (top right), the Sumatran Tupai (bottom right) and a turtle (bottom left). Facing page: The birds too, are depicted in fine detail. These illustrations show just a few of Indonesia's 1,600 species, more than a sixth of the world's total bird population.*

*The Balinese have shown the ultimate rejection of foreign usurpers in a series of cataclysmic ritual suicides. When Dutch troops marched into Denpasar in 1896, they were met by a silent procession of white-clad Balinese led by their Rajah, who systematically began to stab themselves to death in front of the astonished troops.*

*W*hat a shame photography was not used in the days of the early European explorers. This romanticised depiction of Kalimantan Dayak warriors strays a little from reality, especially the ritual tattoos.

*Rites of passage are celebrated throughout Indonesia, especially those involving circumcision (as in this Sulawesi group). Occasions such as this provide an opportunity for pomp and finery, even in the simple villages.*

*The Dutch travelled in fine, if slow style during their occupation of Indonesia. Women sat in palanquins carried on the shoulders of Javanese coolies (top). The Dutch lived in style in large households filled with servants. They took up the practice of wearing batik sarong or pants while lounging about the house during their leisure hours (bottom).*

*Beloved by generations of anthropologists and ethnographers, the Nias warriors epitomised the "noble savage" that they idealised. Both their exotic costumes, houses and extraordinary megalithic culture made study of their customs most rewarding (above and facing page).*

*Looking a little like an oriental version of Queen Victoria, the wife of the Sultan of Deli poses with her husband. This sultanate of North Sumatra was once as lavish as the courts of Java at its peak.*

NOTE: HE IS MY GREAT GREAT GRAND FATHER (PAKUBUWONO X)

*Looking every inch a sultan, the imperious Sultan of Surakarta poses with his family dressed in fine robes of more than a touch of European influence as shown in his tight-fitting jacket.*

LUKI

*In the realms of classical dance, nothing changes very much. These portraits of Surakata classical dancers taken more than a century ago can barely be distinguished from a modern dance. It is only the style of photography that changes (above and facing page).*

*The dress of the Balinese too has changed little, except that the T-shirts, too often employed, are accompanied by a certain loss of grace.*